MW01635685

THIS KITCHEN IS FOR DANCING

REAL FOOD, PURE FLAVOR

OVER 100 DELICIOUS & HEALTHY RECIPES

KARLENE KARST

Dedication

To my husband Gaetano, and my three children Luca, Matteo, and Capri.
You are the greatest gift and accomplishment in my life.
Everything I do, I do for you. May you continue to grow with the love
and respect for nourishing your body with healthy, real, and pure food,
while enjoying the joy and dance in the kitchen.

Love, your mama XO

THIS KITCHEN IS FOR DANCING

REAL FOOD, PURE FLAVOR

mind
PUBLISHING

For information contact:

Mind Publishing Inc.
PO Box 57559,
1031 Brunette Avenue
Coquitlam, BC Canada V3K 1E0
Tel: 604-777-4330 Toll free: 1-877-477-4904
Fax: 1-866-367-5508
Email: info@mindpublishing.com
mindpublishing.com

ISBN: 978-1-927017-31-9

Printed in Canada

Art Direction/Design: Stephen Rank, Beata Stolarska

Cover and Food Photography: Tracey Ayton Photography, *@tracey_ayton*

Back Cover Photography: Tonino Guzzo, *@toninoguzzo*

Additional Photography: Brooklyn D Photography, *@brooklyndphotography*

Food Styling, Creative and Recipe Collaboration:
Yassi Kazemi, *@lovenourishinspire*

Content Editor: Nancy Cheeseman

Copy Editor: Brinda Navjee

Biography

Karlene Karst holds a BSc in nutrition and is a leading authority in natural health and wellness. She is the founder of the award-winning brand Sea-licious® Omega-3 oils and has published numerous health books. Karlene is an upbeat, well-informed sought-after TV personality and spokesperson appearing on the cover of magazines and TV shows including *The Marilyn Denis Show, CTV Morning Live, Global Morning News,* and *Breakfast TV.* Karlene is an enthusiastic recipe and food innovator who inspires with her belief in real, whole food as she feeds her busy family of five.

You can follow her daily healthy living tips on Facebook and Instagram *@karlenekarst*

Acknowledgments

Eating has never been so complicated. We are living in a world of abundance of information and choices, which is incredible and overwhelming at the same time! The answer? Simplify. Food should be nourishing in every way of the word, and in this noisy world we live in, it's easy to forget that the best things in life are indeed the most simple. Eating wholesome food, as close to its natural state as possible, in good company is one of life's greatest joys. Cooking doesn't have to be complicated, which is what this book is all about. Making your own food is probably the single-most impactful thing that you can do for youself and your family to help improve their nutrition, and it doesn't have to be difficult or time consuming as Karlene shows you in the pages to follow. So, flip to a page, find something new, and throw on that apron! I know I will! Thank you Karlene for sharing your expertise and delicious recipes with the world!

Tori Weszer, RD
@fraichenutrition

Table of Contents

Preface – This Kitchen Is for Dancing – Real Food, Pure Flavor 9

Chapter One – From Sickness to Health... to Dancing in My Kitchen! 11

Chapter Two – Mom the Heart of the Home: Tips for Self-Care 15

Chapter Three – A Healthy Home Is a Happy Home 19

Chapter Four – Meal Prep Is Easy, Efficient, and Fun! 27

Chapter Five – The Real Food Pantry 35

Chapter Six – Recipes

- Breakfast 51
- Snacks 93
- Soup 119
- Veggies 147
- Weekday Dinner 197
- Sunday Dinner 237
- Sweet Treats 261

Chapter Seven – Resource Guide 292

Index 293

GF = GLUTEN FREE V = VEGAN DF = DAIRY FREE

This Kitchen Is for Dancing

Real Food, Pure Flavor

It's such an honor to have the opportunity to share with you my journey of food, nutrition, and finding my best health. *This Kitchen Is for Dancing – Real Food, Pure Flavor* has been such a labor of love! I cannot wait for you to try the meal-planning techniques and the easy and delicious recipes you will find in this book. I hope that they will not only help nourish you and your family, but also provide you new opportunities to gather around the table, share the day's moments of joy, and to make memories that will last forever.

I believe it: your kitchen should be for dancing! Cooking shouldn't be a chore, and finding time to share love and joy over a dining table with your family – well, it deserves to be a priority in your hectic life.

You might wonder if I'm going to teach you how to cook in this book? No, and here's why. There's no right or wrong way to cook! What matters is the care you bring to it. Of course, some of us are naturally better at combining ingredients or more skilled in kitchen techniques. But I'm here to say it doesn't matter, not in the final analysis. If you love your family enough to feed them healthy food – and I know you do – you will cook well. I know this in my heart. If you're willing to put your heart and soul into the task every time you walk into the kitchen, the results are sure to please your family, and you, too! That's because you've combined your fresh, healthy ingredients with the one component that's indispensable: love. It's what makes the difference between seeing cooking as a burden, and seeing it as the happy dance it ought to be.

What I do want to do instead, in this book, is to poke a few pins into the idea that cooking, especially for a family is difficult. It's a challenge, of course, but there are ways to make the job a lot easier. This book will tell you how to stock your pantry and freezer for maximum versatility and flexibility in your meal planning. I'll provide you shopping tips and a complete guide to not just survive weekly meal prepping for faster meals on the busiest days, but also show you how to make it a bonding time for your family. I'll also show you how to develop practical, inspiring philosophies of food and living to guide you day in and day out.

With building blocks such as these in place, your kitchen will become yours to dance in. Maybe not every meal you put on the table will bring you joy – there are some days, as we all know when you have to get it done. But my own experience tells me that as you grow in confidence regarding what it takes to feed your family healthy, nutritious food, you will also gain a deepening sense of satisfaction. You'll know you're doing your best for your family, by helping each member to stay healthy and energetic. You'll also discover that your kitchen isn't just the place where the food is, it's honestly the center of your home – it is the heart of your life!

WHAT YOU'LL FIND IN THE UPCOMING CHAPTERS

As you read on, I'll show you how I manage to put some basic principles to work in my family's everyday life. Each chapter is packed with information to help you establish your own goals and guidelines, to enhance your recipe selection, shop for the healthiest ingredients, and develop some personal and organizational strategies to make it all fit with the busy life you lead.

- In **Chapter One,** I tell you my story, my "food journey," and why my kitchen is a place for dancing.

- In **Chapter Two,** I recognize what we all know to be true. Everything depends on Mom – the family is only healthy and happy to the extent she is.
- In **Chapter Three,** I delve deeper into what it takes to create and maintain a healthy kitchen and a happier and more comfortable home.
- **Chapter Four** is an important chapter. Many busy families either underestimate the importance of meal prepping or they aren't sure how to make it work with their schedules. That's why I devoted an entire chapter to teaching you how to make meal prepping quick and easy. I think you'll find great benefit in the information, as I'm continually hearing from busy parents and singles that meal prepping has completely changed the game for them when it comes to eating real food.
- **Chapter Five** is a comprehensive resource guide you'll need for making every bite count in your kitchen. It contains everything you'd want to know about how to stock your fridge and pantry. Also, every ingredient and tool I commonly use in my kitchen is listed there. If you see something in a recipe that you're not sure of, this section is your friend!
- In **Chapter Six,** I've lovingly created over 100 healthy, real food recipes that my friends and family have been gracious enough to test, taste, and review for me. And I can tell you, no one is more honest or critical than three grade-schoolers, so I'm confident that you'll enjoy every one of these recipes. I offer them knowing not only that you'll find them healthy and delicious, but that they'll inspire you to start or continue that beautiful dance in your kitchen!

Let's dance on!

Chapter One

From Sickness to Health... to Dancing in My Kitchen!

Healthy practices, the kind that leads to a happier and more vital life, don't arrive magically overnight. We don't change or improve with a snap of the fingers. Things take time and effort, and success almost always comes with setbacks. With good examples to follow, strong reasons to make a change, and plenty of support along the way, we get where we need to go. We change. We improve.

All of this is my way of saying: Don't think I just waved a wand and, poof, I knew how to cook well, serve healthy food, and find joy in the everyday rhythm of feeding my family. Far from it! However I did have plenty of motivation to get me started in the right direction, as you'll soon learn. And I benefited from the best of examples, my mother and later, my husband's joyful, fun, food-loving Italian family!

Growing up on a farm in Saskatchewan, Canada, my mother instilled in me strong family and food values. I watched her lovingly feed our family, every night, with home-cooked meals. (There was no such thing as takeout sushi in rural Saskatchewan in the 1980s.)

I can't say I fully appreciated my mother's healthy meals at the time. I have to admit; I was often envious of my friends who were allowed to enjoy toaster pastries and pizza pockets – which were then the novelties of the grocery store's prepared- and frozen-food aisles. Now, looking back, I'm so very grateful for the warm, healthy meals my mother laid out for us. They set the foundation for my love of home-cooked food and spending time in the kitchen. Even more importantly, those happy times around the dinner table taught me that mama's cooking is not only good for the body, it also sustains the soul.

Today in my own home, I strive to achieve a philosophy similar to my mother's. I regularly cook, as my mother did. It is a fact that life with three kids can be crazy with its ups and downs, but preparing for meals in advance makes cooking dinner each night more pleasant. No last-minute decisions or running to the store. I find the simple acts of organizing ingredients, chopping, and stirring very fulfilling. It gives me time to take a break from my computer and the stresses of my day. By the time my kids and husband come through the door, I'm able to sit back, eat, and enjoy my family.

I don't want to overwork the idea of dancing, though there are some similarities between learning to dance and learning to feed one's family with joy. First, you appreciate the dancing that you see and experience – just as I did with my mother's cooking. Then, you want to try a few moves, to learn some steps, whether that's in a kitchen or on a dance floor. It's hard at first, mostly because it's all so unfamiliar. In spite of this, you still gain confidence from your gradual improvement. You keep trying. As a result, you get better. Gradually, it becomes fun!

That's how it's been for me, a life-long journey of learning and improving. I would be remiss if I didn't tell you where a great deal of my motivation came from. I want to say it was the sheer excitement of learning new skills to benefit my family. Especially in recent years, there's been plenty of that kind of motivation. However, earlier in my life, I found my food odyssey spurred on by a particular fear. I had become frightened of what my life would be like if I didn't figure out how to restore my health.

My late teens were a very difficult time for me. My father died of cancer in 1995, and losing him proved pivotal in many unfortunate ways. Most importantly, my health took a turn for the worse as I began suffering from continual pain and inflammation – which I now know was the result of years of chronic stress impacting my gastrointestinal tract. Acutely aware that something wasn't right, I visited doctor after doctor until finally, at age 20, I was diagnosed with an autoimmune condition called mixed connective tissue disease. According to the medical practice of the time, I was prescribed drugs to combat the inflammation, which in turn caused dangerous side effects. Unfortunately there was one thing the drugs didn't do – reduce my pain.

During this time, I thought I was eating healthily. I was on a low-fat diet, which in that era was believed to be the healthiest way to eat. However, we now know that such diets allow for plenty of packaged and processed foods, many of which lack nutrients and are high in sugar content. Even though I looked good, fit and trim, I was starving myself of the very nutrients my body needed most, to cope with my autoimmune condition and the pain caused by inflammation.

One day, a thought struck me like an arrow: "If this was how I felt in my twenties, how bad would I feel in my forties?"

Thankfully, this became a real "aha" moment. Soon, by reading and studying, I learned that food indeed has the power to heal. And thus, my nutrition journey began. By 1999, I became a nutritionist and embraced the growing movement toward health and healing through food. I committed myself to not just eating, but indeed feeding my body with the nutrients and fiber it needs to function at its best.

Fast-forward to now, more than two decades later: I feel AMAZING and empowered! My food journey continues, of course, nonetheless it has evolved in an extraordinary way. Now I'm not just feeding myself, I also work daily to feed my family, always striving to instill healthy core values about food in my children.

As many of you, women, might know, becoming a mother truly tests us in every possible way. And also like many of you, I consider my biggest and best accomplishment to be – well, believe it or not – it's not regaining my health or building a thriving business in the natural health field, it's being a mom to three healthy, active, kind, and beautiful children. Feeding them nutritious food is one of the ways that I share my love with them, and with my husband as well. I'm not good at crafts, drawing, or painting. I maintain an active lifestyle through walking, hiking, barre fitness, and full-body training along with many beautiful friendships that inspire me to be a better mom and wife. However, where I devote a significant amount of my time and attention, aside from being the CEO of my brand and business, is in my kitchen.

You and I know that it's not easy in today's world when working at a job outside the home, raising kids, taking care of a house and yard, nurturing friendships and extended family relationships, engaging the kids in sports and activities, and oh, by the way, keeping yourself strong and healthy. I'm somehow doing it, as most of us are. The life I've chosen means I'm going from 5:00 AM to 10:00 PM almost daily, and I can honestly say it's been the most complicated "dance" of my life. When I reminisce my twenties when I thought I was busy – well, I was, however I wasn't caring for four other people besides myself! Things have certainly speeded up and gotten more complicated over the years, and I can honestly say I feel energized, capable, and, above all, truly happy. I consciously pat myself on the back for finding so much enjoyment, especially while working hard. I can't believe how I've adapted to this crazy, yet beautiful life of mine!

In all of life, motherhood stands alone in the adaptation it requires of us. Yes, getting educated for a career is tough. Establishing yourself in a job or a profession can be challenging. Getting married and adjusting to sharing time and space with someone else is equally hard. Nonetheless, there's absolutely nothing that causes the same magnitude of required adaptation as having children. As soon as I had little ones to raise, my dance in the kitchen needed to change dramatically to accommodate their needs. Making nourishing, real food wasn't enough anymore. I also had to figure out: (1) how to make food that tastes great to their little taste buds, and (2) how to make it quick, easy, and (sometimes sneakily) nutritious.

For the past decade, I've navigated just about every food challenge possible, from picky eaters, with their strong likes and dislikes, to food sensitivities, to those perpetually hungry teens with their on-the-go eating. There have been birthday parties, play dates, and so many school lunches. I am the chief cook in our family and the majority of days I need to have dinner made and the kids fed long before my husband gets home from work. Some days we eat in shifts because of after-school sports schedules. Some days I'm stressed and impatient, although I feel proud and brave that I take such a passionate interest in feeding my family under not-always-easy circumstances and courageous for committing to this while also working. I feel grateful, too, to have been able to "dance" my way through over 10 years of feeding my family.

I often think of what Darwin said: "It's not the strongest or the smartest who survive; it's those who can adapt." And, adapt I have!

Still, having a kitchen for dancing is much more than getting healthy food on the table meal after meal, day after day, so much more! It's about creating a safe, nurturing place for the family. It's also about shared experiences, whether cooking together, laughing together, crying together, or making plans together. A kitchen is a place for not just nourishment through food, but also emotional and spiritual nourishment. It's where our children make their deepest, longest-lasting memories.

Think I'm exaggerating? Consider: A family's key moments tend to occur in the kitchen. There, we experience the laughter, the meltdowns, the celebrations, the sorrows, and the prayers. Moments like these, big and small, are what shape our lives. So, when I say my kitchen is for dancing, it's really about the dance of life that occurs while feeding the people you love.

It's vital for me to note that my understanding of the kitchen as the heart of the home was enhanced by marrying into an Italian family. My husband's heritage has introduced me to a culture that embraces wholesome, fresh, and real food – yes, of course! As a matter of fact, for Italians, food is so much more than this. Food represents the good life. It's the smell of cooking, the chatter of children, the clatter of knives and dishes, the burst of a song (in our house it's Michael Bublé singing jazz standards), and the often wordless coordination of people working together who truly care about each other. Yes, my husband's Italian culture has entirely shown me that we feed a family best when we also nourish it with love and time spent together.

FOOD AND LOVE – ISN'T THAT THE VERY DEFINITION OF HAVING A ZEST FOR LIFE?

As you'll see in chapters to come, I'm a firm believer in superfoods and beneficial supplements such as my omega-3 brand Sea-licious®. In the recipes I provide, I try to make every bite count, nutritionally speaking. Yet, my family's food philosophy is simple: we keep it wholesome, real, pure, and flavorful, and always uncomplicated. We still enjoy sweet treats like muffins and cakes, yet in moderation and only when made with nutritious flours like spelt or oat. We use fat in everything and focus on avocado, coconut and extra virgin olive oils, rather than processed and refined oils.

I believe that going back to the basics of food and nutrition, and cooking at home does more than restore our health. It creates a routine that helps transition us from our busy days to a cozy and calm place at evening time. The kitchen then becomes a place to pause and reflect together on our shared priorities and values.

In a busy world, creating a family cocoon of the kind I'm describing isn't easy. It takes commitment and a willingness to set standards to safeguard your family's ability to gather over food. For me, a fundamental responsibility and a family standard are that we will always have a special Sunday together. Other than church in the morning, I have tried to make Sundays a day where we don't commit to outings or extra-curricular events. I take it seriously enough that I won't schedule any sports or activities for the kids on Sundays. Instead, I make Sunday dinner the focus of the entire day. It's an opportunity to get the kids involved in the kitchen, to cook something a little more elaborate, or to try a unique cut of meat such as lamb. For these occasions, I enjoy setting the dinner table with a beautiful linen tablecloth, candles, cloth napkins and, of course, a favorite bottle of wine. If I'm feeling extra ambitious, I may even make a dessert. One key point, though is that this special time does not have to happen on Sunday. Reserve any night of the week you choose! The goal is merely to gather as a family for a special meal on a regular basis – one that can be safe from interruption and dependably held week after week.

What I've learned in my food journey is that food heals, not just nutritionally, but just about in every other way possible! Food connects and reconnects us to one another. Food shared at a table reminds us of our past and helps us discover our future. Yes, it matters what we eat – very much so! It also matters where and how. The social and emotional impact of working together to eat together is what makes any kitchen one for dancing.

Gathering around the table to break bread, share conversations and stories has been a time-honored tradition since time began. My sincerest goal for you and your loved ones in writing *This Kitchen Is for Dancing – Real Food, Pure Flavor* is to take you back to a simpler place, a kinder place, and a gentler time. Now let's begin looking at how you can create such a kitchen in your home!

Chapter Two

Mom the Heart of the Home: Tips for Self-Care

As a mom and advocate of healthy family living, I often get asked if there's such a thing as a work-life balance. Is achieving it possible? Or is it just a media myth? I haven't mastered it yet, but hey, as long as I'm alive, there's still time! What I can say is that I try to be strategic with my energy, and I strive to create time for pleasure as well as for self-care. (I love an aromatherapy bath at the end of the day!). Ultimately, because I'm incredibly passionate about both my work and my family, I find ways of making it all function, and that's because I believe in the saying: "If Mom isn't happy, nobody's happy!" Below are my tips for balancing a busy life while still finding time to care for yourself.

FINDING GRATITUDE

The practice of gratitude is a powerful one, and the benefits are nearly endless, as I'm sure you know. However, living a tradition like this can be difficult in more ways than one with life's fits and starts, especially given our busy daily lives. A couple of years ago, I made a pact with myself that each morning I would wake up a little earlier to allow time for journaling, gratitude, and prayer. It's a relatively small thing, yet so powerful and maybe for that reason, I have managed to stick with it. Some mornings my gratitude is limited to merely having coffee in the house and being thankful for another day! Other mornings it flows from me almost unceasingly. One thing that is never missing from my prayers and meditation, though, is gratitude for my health. Without it, I wouldn't be able to enjoy all the gifts in my life entirely. Knowing so deeply what it's like to be unhealthy, I cannot help, but be grateful for my health.

Gratitude works! When we're on a journey to reach an improved or optimal health, or to straighten out problems in our lives, we tend to focus on what isn't right, or why we aren't feeling good. Focusing on the negative can leave us feeling down. In these cases, research indicates that expressing feelings of gratitude can improve our overall enjoyment of life, as well as our health and happiness. So, instead of focusing on what's not right, it's better to zero-in on the one (or more) components of your life that you're blessed to have. Indeed, I encourage you to try a 30-day gratitude project, where each day you write down three things you're grateful for every day. Write it down in a journal, and along with these thoughts, write down how you're feeling. It's a fantastic practice to help you become more aware of how your mood, energy, and ideas about life shift throughout the process.

PRACTICING MINDFULNESS

The practice of focusing on things happening in the present moment, like the sounds, smells, and thoughts going through your mind, is a great way to calm your inner monologue and allow you to appreciate each moment. "Be present now," some say. Well, just like gratitude, mindfulness works. When we turn inwards and tune into our surroundings, studies show that we have the power to relieve stress, pain, and even illness.

Mindfulness translates to food as well. We're all so spoiled with such a variety of food available to us. It's always best to choose the real food and savor it. Due to our tendency to overconsume boxed and processed foods, we begin to lose our pleasure and enjoyment of eating. Besides, our busy lifestyles keep us in too much of a hurry to sit down, relax, and enjoy our meals. Of course, I do get it, it can be difficult to mindfully sit down and notice the aromas and tastes of the food set before you, especially with children chattering and our continual need to be getting up for a glass, a fork, more water, whatever. But, to the extent we can, being mindful when eating will improve digestion, nutrient absorption, gut health, and serotonin release. Overall, mindfulness decreases stress and helps us climb a step or two higher on our happiness index. Try putting your phone down and living your best life instead of watching someone else live their life on a mobile device – is a great start.

OPTIMIZING NUTRITION

Take it to the bank. What we put in our bodies every single day influences how we feel. Studies have proven the link between food and well-being. Food is power. Food is fuel. Food is health. Indeed, it's impossible to talk about improving our health without talking about real, fresh food. To improve health, we must begin by making the right food choices. I understand that it can be overwhelming to know which changes to make in your diet. There are so many ingredients and additives as well as preservatives to be aware of in all packaged foods! Before you begin making changes to your diet, it may pay to take some time to become familiar with all the new ingredients, restock your pantry, and re-organize your fridge. That's why I created a chapter, coming later, that will help you restock your pantry and fridge and, of course, 100+ delicious, nourishing and simple recipes to help get you started.

MAKING YOURSELF A PRIORITY

Motherhood is indeed the most selfless thing you can do in your life. My first intuition is to always help my kids before doing anything just for me, however I encourage all of us to be kind – better – to ourselves. Fill your cup so that you feel you have something to share. When you feel energized and passionate, you're better able to take care of your family. Go for a coffee date with a friend, set aside a date night with your spouse, take a yoga class on a Saturday morning – whatever activity boosts your spirit, do it. Everyone in your family will reap the benefits of a happy, healthy mom.

Along with a good self-care routine comes the importance of setting boundaries and being able to say "no." Over the years, I've had to learn this art. As I've done so, it's helped us find more balance as a family, because I'm no longer overcommitting myself. Another important boundary comes from making it a practice to disconnect from electronic devices at 9:00 PM each night or earlier. I turn my phone to airplane mode and leave it in a different part of the house before bed. We also shut off the Wi-Fi to give our brains a chance to relax. These may be little things, yet they all contribute to our well-being.

ESTABLISHING A MORNING ROUTINE

Being both a mom and a "mom-preneur," I've formed habits over the years that help me stay focused when I'm being pulled in all directions. I rely on my morning routine, which sets the stage for the day. It may be hard at first to find what kind of routine works well enough for you to stick to it, but believe me, once you find it, it's a lifesaver.

I genuinely believe that habits are the underlying force behind overall success in life. In addition, I think that happiness and satisfaction in family, food, career, faith, and friendships also stem from setting and maintaining healthy, useful habits. Don't expect to roll out a specific routine from the start, however. My suggestion is to start small and make developing your routine so easy that it can't help, but stick. Then, work on increasing new habits in small ways to eventually create a morning routine that gives you energy and prepares you for the day ahead.

I was born and raised to be an early riser, that's the farmer in me. Even during my university days, I couldn't make myself sleep in. I have an internal clock that wakes me before the sun rises. And that's a good thing because a study published in The American Psychological Association journal *Emotion* reports early risers are happier, healthier, and more productive than night owls.

If you're working towards getting an earlier start in the mornings, it's important to remember that you still need your seven to eight hours of sleep. I get up at 5:00 AM each workday morning, so going to bed early is crucial if I'm going to log the amount of sleep my body needs before I get up. If you're struggling to create a morning routine, here are my favorite tips and tricks:

1. **Prime the pump!** While you may love your early morning coffee or tea, before you dive in, begin each day with a big glass of lemon water. Many of us are very dehydrated first thing in the morning, and water with lemon helps flush out toxins, rehydrate the body, and improve digestion.
2. **Next, take the time to practice gratitude, prayer, or meditation.** My faith has always been my steadfast guide, and although I find

myself praying throughout the day, I start my morning mindfully expressing my feelings of gratitude and thanks. Get in the habit of writing down three things you're grateful for, as well as three goals for the day. Research shows that by recording just three tasks, and then achieving them, you will feel more accomplished, have greater satisfaction and get more tasks done throughout the day.

3 **Take time to read the news or something educational.** It is important to feel connected to world events and your community. Or, maybe you want to study up on something interesting from the history of the arts? For me, it's the newspaper. I have it delivered to my front door every morning, and I LOVE It! I love the tangible feeling of print on paper; it's the perfect accompaniment to my morning coffee. Sometimes I can only afford to spend 10 minutes going over the news, but at least I feel caught up with what's happening.

4 **Another essential task I regularly incorporate into my morning routine is exercise.** With such a busy family life, getting in a little time to be active is crucial, so I carve out at least two days per week when I can get some exercise in the morning. Research shows that we reap greater mental and physical benefits from exercise when it's done at the beginning of the day compared to the end of the day. I love the increased focus and positivity I feel. I also notice decreased symptoms of stress associated with my workouts, not to mention greater ease in maintaining a healthy weight.

5 **Finally, my most important tip is never to skip breakfast.** Breakfast breaks the fast from the night before. Your body needs nutrition first thing in the morning. Ideally, you should eat within 30–60 minutes of waking up, and always include 20–25 g of protein. Protein nourishes the adrenal glands, helping to reduce sugar cravings and boosting your metabolism so that you're able to deal with stress more effectively throughout the day.

When it comes to morning nourishment, skip the sugar-laden cereals, and switch to nutritious green smoothies with protein powder, eggs, Greek yogurt, nut butters, nuts and seeds, or steel-cut oats. By making use of the breakfast options I've included in this book, you'll be starting your day off on the right foot. Focusing on these healthy alternatives will not only fuel your body and reduce your sugar intake and cravings, but it will also do the same for other members of your family at the same time.

Okay, now you're ready to drill deeper into the tips and techniques that will bring joy, harmony, and efficiency into your kitchen routines!

Chapter Three

A Healthy Home Is a Happy Home

My journey of self-discovery and finding my balance in life has led to many food and lifestyle changes over the years. From seeing and noticing the effects of good fats on my well-being to decreasing how much sugar I consume, to ditching processed food and incorporating more mindfulness, relaxation, and family time, I've learned so much. I can honestly say that I've found the "diet" that works best for my body – and it's a far cry from the low-fat diet that led me to be such a deprived, depressed, and unhealthy girl in the 1990s.

I've now reached a point where I feel amazing in my body, and I know what nourishes my family and me. Perhaps it's my Swedish roots or just the balanced harmony I look for in the universe, but the key principle of *lagom,* Swedish word meaning "just a little, not too much," is the way I live my life. I've come to find a balance in a hybrid of Mediterranean living – lots of whole, real food, a focus on fresh vegetables, healthy fats and, of course, a glass of wine with dinner – that's my jam! Over the years I've compiled a collection of knowledge to guide me in my food and lifestyle choices, and I'd like to share them with you – in the hope that they will guide you or inspire you to find a balance that genuinely works for you.

QUALITY OVER QUANTITY

I believe the only way to truly nourish your body is to focus on this basic philosophy: "Pay more attention to the quality of your food than the quantity." It may seem scary at first, however, rather than counting calories and measuring serving sizes, I recommend focusing on eating good quality, organic, whole, real food. Listen to your body and apply the principle of *lagom* in your life – not too much, not too little, and just enough – of the right stuff.

THE BODY KNOWS

Listening to your body is a skill we've sadly lost over the years. Many of us are too focused on the numbers – achieving a specific weight loss goal, or doggedly following the current diet craze. We forget that our bodies know best. Your body will signal to you when it's full or when a particular type of food disagrees with it; you have to learn to listen again.

Of course, it's likely been so long since you've felt your absolute best that you've probably forgotten how to react. If that's true, a process of reconnecting with your intuition is what's needed. Once you see how good you can genuinely feel without the worrying, calorie counting, and self-judging, you'll be able to assess better how certain food transforms you physically, mentally, and even emotionally. Think what this means for your family, too. Might each family member look and feel better if they were eating healthy, real food? Might they also learn to listen to their bodies?

SPEND TIME TOGETHER

Your family's health depends on more than just the food you eat. Spending time together, enjoying the outdoors, getting daily exercise, and laughing, talking, and bonding over a delicious meal is crucial to not just your overall happiness, but ultimately to your health. I'm a massive advocate of setting one day a week aside to sit down together, cook a family meal, open a bottle of wine for the grownups, and talk about your day and the things that are important to you.

FOCUS ON THE JOURNEY

There is no one day or one meal that you can eat or not eat, to change the course of your health and well-being. This journey you're on is about small, consistent steps in the right direction, ones that add up to significant results. If you feel like you've failed, forgive yourself. We all make the occasional mistake. I know I have, and with so many things to juggle and take care of, it's tough always to be the perfect parent, partner, and person. When a child falls, we hug them. Why don't we do the equivalent for ourselves? So, my advice is to accept that this is a journey and a process. Do the best you can. Every step you take in the right direction is, in itself, a success.

REAL HOMEMADE FOOD IS HEALTHIER

I know there are many demands on you and you're stretched thin. The thought of regularly cooking meals at home may seem daunting. Trust me, I've worked hard to keep all the recipes in this book as simple and delicious as possible. They work for my busy family, and I believe they can work for yours, too. Taking time to cook real, nourishing food is an investment in your family's future.

Instead of reaching for prepared meals, spend a little time doing prep work in the kitchen so that you can reap the rewards later on. Elsewhere in this book, I give you all of my favorite tips and tricks to making meal prep easy, practical, and fun. "Chore no more" – preparing meals for the week can and will become a family activity for everyone to enjoy!

By eating at home, you've already won half the nutrition battle. The meals you prepare for your family at home will be a lot healthier than anything you could order off a menu. Plus you'll know what's going into your food. Making most of the food your family eats at home is a big and important step towards overall health.

CHOOSE WHOLE, REAL FOOD

When we're talking about whole, real food, what we mean is food in their most natural state – fruit, vegetables, whole grains, nuts, seeds, legumes, and if you choose to include them, dairy and sustainably sourced meat, poultry, and seafood.

When I think about fueling my body, I think about a quote from famous food author, journalist, and activist, Michael Pollen, "If it came from a plant, eat it; if it was made in a plant, don't." When we consume processed food made in factories and laboratories, our bodies don't recognize these substances as nourishment. During regular digestion, the body breaks down the food we eat into nutrients and absorbs these for energy and well-being. When it comes to processed food, the preservatives, artificial sweeteners, fake colors, and numerous other food-like substances in these products, are foreign and classified as toxic by the body. These processed food place a severe burden on the often already overworked digestive and detoxification systems.

Besides, some of these compounds are too toxic for the body to eliminate. Instead, they get packaged up safely into bundles that are stored in fatty tissue deposits for safe-keeping until the body has time and energy to deal with them. The more we eat these types of food, the more fatty tissue is needed to store them, leading to weight gain and cellulite formation.

Whole, real, fresh food is a vital component of a healthy lifestyle – we can go even one step further. To ensure that we're getting the maximum amount of nutrients, while also taking care of the planet and supporting the people who work so hard to grow and harvest our food, we need to be able to recognize and understand the various certifications and labeling.

BECOME LABEL LITERATE

Let's dive a little deeper into labels like organic, local, grass fed, non-GMO, sustainably farmed, antibiotic and hormone free, free range and pasture raised, so that next time you're at the grocery store, you can figure out what the best options are for you and your loved ones.

WHEN SELECTING PRODUCE

Local. Where and how my food is grown is important to me, that's why I'm such a huge fan of visiting my local farmers' market. This a weekly family outing we always look forward to. I also love supporting my local community and talking directly to the farmers who grow and raise my food. Purchasing local produce also ensures that I get the freshest, healthiest, and most delicious produce available. I believe it's one of the best ways to reconnect with the farms where our food comes from.

Farmers work so hard day in and day out to produce a wide assortment of nutritious ingredients. Most of the produce sold at the farmers' market was picked that very morning, in its most ripe and nutrient-dense state – while food purchased at the grocery store has often traveled hundreds, if not thousands, of miles, to get to the store. Grocery store produce is also often picked before it's ripe and sprayed with chemicals to speed up ripening before it's placed on grocery store shelves. This results in produce that is not at its peak nutrition and creates an unsustainable process for our planet.

Next time you're at the farmers' market, don't be shy. Farmers love to talk about their harvest proudly. Chat with your local farmers and ask them what farming practices they use, whether they spray their crops with any pesticides or herbicides, and if not, what kind of pest control measures are used. Ask them if they use GMO seeds, and whether they hold any certifications. This way you'll be able to tell if you're getting the best-quality, local, organic food.

Organic (and non-GMO). While local often means organic, it isn't always so. It's also important to remember that a farm may use organic farming practices without being certified organic. This is often the case with small farms that don't have the budget or time resources to seek official certifications.

You can discover this by speaking directly with the farmers. You can also ask them if you can visit their farm. Farmers are often more than happy to have you stop by and visit.

Another critical component of organic farming is the banning of GMO or genetically modified organisms. GMO crops have been genetically modified using DNA from other species to make the plants more resilient to pests, disease, and drought as well as boosting yield. This type of genetic modification is so new that many argue that its effects on humans and animals are unknown. Buying organic produce ensures that NO GMO seeds and plants are getting onto your plate.

However, if you're not able to buy organic (due to lack of availability, price, season etc.), you can implement effective washing strategies such as using a 3:1 dilution of water and vinegar which can remove 90% of waxes, sprays, and dirt that may be lingering on your produce. Always spend the extra time to properly clean your produce.

WHEN IT COMES TO MEAT AND ANIMAL PRODUCTS...

For my loved ones, I take extra care to select grass-fed, sustainable, humanely raised and butchered meat and animal products – and ones that are antibiotic and hormone free. This is a kind and environmentally conscious approach to buying meat and animal products, and it's also essential for the long-term health of my family.

Hormone and antibiotic free. It may be tough at first to find hormone- and antibiotic-free meat at traditional big-box grocery stores, nonetheless more and more retailers are taking notice of demand and stocking these better-quality products. Be sure to ask around and make connections. Soon you'll meet other like-minded individuals and butchers who are doing it right, and you'll have access to new ways of sourcing your meat.

Buying your meat from farmers who use natural farming practices is not only good for the animals and the environment, but also beneficial for your health. Firstly, grass-fed beef is higher in nutrients, and secondly, they don't have any of the antibiotics and hormones that are conventionally fed to animals in order to store fat in their cells. We literally become what we eat, and if we're eating hormones and antibiotics then those chemicals get incorporated into our bodies. To get the cleanest, most natural and nourishing meat products, always select meat raised without the use of hormones and antibiotics.

Free range, pasture raised, and grass fed. While many people are familiar with the importance of eliminating hormones and antibiotics, other classifications can be more confusing. I often get asked to explain the difference between free range, pasture raised, and grass fed. What does it mean for the animals and our well-being?

To keep things simple, grass fed is best when it comes to livestock, poultry, and eggs. For ruminant animals, like cows, goats, and sheep, grass-fed means they have been sustained only on their mother's milk, fresh grass, and grass-type hay for their entire lives. They have enjoyed the great outdoors and have grazed naturally.

Similarly, pasture-raised animals are also given ample space to roam outside, often on organically managed pastures. The main difference is that these animals eat supplemental grains. Studies show that meat from animals that eat only grass has higher levels of healthy anti-inflammatory omega-3s and vitamin E, as compared to animals that eat grains.

Free-range animals mean they are able to roam freely outside allowing exposure to fresh air, and feeding on natural food sources such as grass.

Humane. An additional certification of "humane" is added to any of the above categories, which indicates that the animals are provided with a minimum amount of space per animal. Depending on the designation, this can be anywhere from 1.5 sq ft per animal when it comes to cage free, to 108 sq ft per animal for pasture raised.

REDUCING THE AMOUNT OF SUGAR YOUR FAMILY EATS

Mindfully managing the amount of sugar we consume is a subject that's particularly near and dear to my heart. I hope you won't mind if we spend a couple of extra minutes discussing this incredibly important topic.

I've seen and experienced sugar's effects on the body firsthand; in my own journey to health, as well as while raising three little ones. Back when I was a young student studying nutrition in the mid-1990s, fat was vilified and eating low-fat and "fat-free everything" was considered the health standard. This meant that much of the food I was eating was packed with sugar and carbohydrates. As I've already told you, I can honestly say it was the unhealthiest I have ever been.

My autoimmune condition was continually flaring up, thanks to the pro-inflammatory nature of sugar. My skin was breaking out. I had little energy, I was plagued with mood swings, and when I didn't feel completely awful, I certainly felt totally blah.

Over the years, I've changed and tweaked my diet and lifestyle to find what suits my body, and one of the most significant changes I made was cutting sugar from my diet. I noticed the effects almost immediately – on my autoimmune symptoms, on my skin, on my energy level, and so much more. It's hard to believe how quickly you can feel the benefits of ditching sugar! One study took a look at the effects of reducing sugar consumption in overweight teenagers and found that after just 10 days of substituting healthy slow-burning starches for sugars, these young adults significantly reduced their blood pressure, lowered their counts of bad cholesterol, improved their insulin levels, and reduced their risk of heart disease.

Of course, cutting out sugar is easier said than done! We all love the taste of it, although it's even more complicated than that. Studies are now revealing just how incredibly addictive sugar is.

You may have heard recent reports that eating sugar stimulates the same areas in the brain as addictive drugs such as cocaine or heroin, but it might be even worse than that. In one animal study, rats worked eight times harder to get sugar than cocaine; and if they were already cocaine addicted, they switched to sugar as their preferred drug when given a choice.

The power that sugar has over us is remarkable. And what's even worse is that we feed large amounts of it to our kids. Reports reveal that while most adults consume close to 22 teaspoons per day, children are getting up to 35 teaspoons per day! For optimum nutrition, I recommended keeping sugar consumption to less than 5 teaspoons per day.

Just imagining 35 or even 22 teaspoons of sugar in a day is staggering – it's quite a pile! And, if you're wondering where all the sugar is coming from, the answer isn't cakes and cookies, it's processed food. Our constant consumption of "convenience food," those quick, go-to food we feed our kids without a second thought while running to soccer or ballet practice, are packed with hidden processed sugar in all its hundreds of molecular forms.

Hidden sugars – it's another reason why I'm such a big advocate of making your food at home. It's not the maple syrup, coconut sugar, and raw honey you add to your recipes at home that's the problem when it comes to our overconsumption of sugar. The real culprit is the hidden added sugar that's in so many food we commonly consider "healthy" – things like low-fat yogurt, pasta sauces, breakfast cereals, pre-made salad dressings, baked goods, sports drinks, sweetened coffee and tea; and of course, desserts and snack treats, and even ketchup contains added sugar!

Large amounts of sugar are leading to all sorts of diseases, including diabetes, insulin resistance, inflammatory auto-immune conditions, high-blood pressure, high cholesterol, heart disease, liver disease, dementia, cancer, and so much more. Plus, sugar encourages the storage of fat leading to weight gain, thus reducing your sugar intake will help you shed those extra pounds, keep your blood sugar balanced, and prevent brain fog, anxiety, mood swings, and energy slumps throughout the day.

When it comes to our little ones, they're even more vulnerable to the effects of excess sugar. Conditions that typically affect adults are now being seen in children as young as two and three. And, with conditions like hyperactivity, ADHD, and childhood obesity on the rise, scientists are starting to make the connection between these conditions and children's overconsumption of sugar.

SUGAR SUBSTITUTES

Now if you're thinking about substituting artificial sweeteners, then stop right there. Sweeteners like *Sweet'n Low, Splenda,* and *Equal,* are just as bad, if not worse for your health. Not only have these compounds proved to be the cause of cancer in animal studies, they can also lead to damage to neurons in the brain, destruction of beneficial gut bacteria, and the development of glucose intolerance.

So how do we combat this sugar epidemic? I hear all the time from fellow busy parents that convenience is key. We don't have enough time to prepare and cook homemade breakfast, lunch, dinner, and snacks. I know it can be overwhelming! That's why my recipes section includes my favorite quick and easy recipes for nourishing oatmeal, chia puddings, energy balls, muffins, one-sheet meals, and so much more. You can break the fast-food cycle. Trust me you can.

To keep the sugar monster away, I suggest balancing your meals and snacks with healthy fat, protein, and fiber to keep you and your family full and your blood sugar stable. And when it comes to treats, I recommend keeping them as an occasional indulgence, always opting for homemade treats made with healthy ingredients that are satisfying to the taste buds and the body.

As you begin working to reduce the amount of sugar your family consumes, remember that it's a process; it doesn't happen overnight. Establishing basic rules around sweet treats and desserts is a great place to start. By discussing the effects of sugar with your kids, you will not only help instill good habits for their future, you will also raise children who understand the connection between what they put into their bodies and how it makes them feel. It's a lesson that many of us adults are still trying to learn!

MY FAMILY FOOD MANAGEMENT PRINCIPLES

Some days, the dance that occurs around the kitchen island is hectic, irritable, and downright unsatisfying. Over the years, I've learned not to aim for beauty or grace in that dance, but rather, flow. It's the flow, the sense that everything is organized and moving forward as it should, that's what gives me confidence and a measure of serenity. Below are some principles that I consider crucial for any family seeking to eat well, stay healthy, and almost always enjoy the togetherness of shared meals.

PLAN AHEAD

Without a plan, we fall victim to the clock and reach for quick meals that come out of boxes or takeout windows. Plan your meals and write down your weekly menu. This will take the anxiety and pressure off of you during the week and ensure you're not scrambling to come up with something on the spot. Do your big grocery shopping on the weekends based on what your menu plan is during the week; pick one day to do a quick run for fresh produce and any other needs that may have come up. This way you won't feel like you're at the grocery store every day.

I can't stress enough how helpful meal planning is for a busy family. That's why I dedicated an entire chapter of this book to proper meal planning. It allows you to only buy what you need for that week, rather than purchasing an assortment of produce or perishable items that will get wasted and thrown out at the end of the week.

BUY IN BULK, COOK IN BATCHES

Buying in bulk is a smart way to feed a family, as it is much more cost-effective. Shop for non-perishable items when they're on sale and stock up. Also remember, frozen produce is just as good as fresh and can be a great alternative in the colder months. Then, when making a recipe, prepare enough to last two meals. If you're making soup, double the recipe. If you're making pancakes on the weekend, double or triple the recipe and freeze the cooked leftovers so that during the week your family can enjoy pancakes or waffles quickly just by putting them in the toaster. My children love popping their pancakes and waffles in the toaster, and so do I!

MAKE BREAKFAST THE NIGHT BEFORE

I love making overnight oats because they're so quick and easy. While we're in the midst of the dinner mess, I quickly make up a few batches to last during the week. It takes under five minutes and then in the morning we have a nourishing breakfast that we can eat at home or take on-the-go to work or school.

GET YOUR KIDS INVOLVED

Depending on their age, give them tasks to do like unloading the dishwasher, setting and clearing the table, or helping to make a quick salad. This helps them feel like they are contributing and will make prep time and clean up much quicker. Getting your kids involved in mealtime will also help raise children who understand the connection between what they put into their bodies and how that makes them feel – something a lot of adults need to learn too.

USE TIME-SAVING APPLIANCES

Use tools like an instant pot or a slow cooker to cut down on active cooking time. Select recipes that don't need a lot of attention, such as soups that cook within 30 minutes, one-sheet dinners, and quick slow cooker chili. They're all designed to feed your family healthfully and with minimal prep time.

THROW OUT THE FOOD "RULES"

In my early twenties, I learned how unhealthy it could be to eat by a specific set of rules. I followed the low-fat, high-sugar, low-protein craze and this left me feeling exhausted, anxious, and in pain. As I started to nourish my body with healthy fats, I could feel my vitality return. This is why I embrace real, whole, unprocessed food. I eat to nourish my body and enjoy my food. I don't worry about portion sizes, instead, I eat until I am full and listen to my body, and I encourage you to do the same. As food author, Michael Pollan says, "Eat food, mostly plants, but not a lot."

ESTABLISH A FAMILY POLICY ON SWEETS

Obesity is a serious issue facing us all. While nobody doesn't enjoy a treat now and then, your family's focus needs to be on keeping these treats as healthy as possible, and occasional rather than regular. Establishing basic rules around treats and desserts will avoid discord and help instill good habits in your kids. It's not necessary to stress the idea of deprivation or restriction, instead focus on the nourishing qualities of healthy food while reserving treats for a nice-to-have instead of a must-have.

GIVE YOURSELF A BREAK

Nothing is going to be perfect. Accept that this is a journey and a process. Do the best you can, forgive yourself for your shortcomings, and remember that every step you take in the right direction represents success. Cooking real food for your family is an investment in your family's future, their health and happiness index, so rather than reaching for prepared meals, spend a little extra time doing some prep so that you can reap the rewards later on. And don't forget that if you're eating at home, you've already won the nutrition battle. The food you prepare for your family at home is going to be a lot healthier than anything you can pull from a package or order off a menu. Committing to making most of the food your family eats from your kitchen is the most important step towards overall health.

References

Intense Sweetness Surpasses Cocaine Reward. *PLoS One*. 2007; 2(8):e698. Published online 2007 Aug 1.

Lim U, Subar AF, Mouw T, et al. Consumption of aspartame-containing beverages and incidence of hematopoietic and brain malignancies. *Cancer Epidemiology, Biomarkers and Prevention*. 2006; 15(9):1654-1659. [PubMed Abstract]

Marinovich M, Galli CL, Bosetti C, et al. Aspartame, low-calorie sweeteners and disease: regulatory safety and epidemiological issues. *Food and Chemical Toxicology*. 2013; 60:109-15. [PubMed Abstract]

National Toxicology Program. NTP report on the toxicology studies of aspartame (CAS No. 22839-47-0) in genetically modified (FVB Tg.AC hemizygous) and B6.129-Cdkn2atm1Rdp (N2) deficient mice and carcinogenicity studies of aspartame in genetically modified [B6.129-Trp53tm1Brd (N5) haploinsufficient] mice (feed studies). *National Toxicology Program genetically modified model report*. 2005; (1):1-222. [PubMed Abstract]

Soffritti M, Belpoggi F, Esposti DD, Lambertini L. Aspartame induces lymphomas and leukaemias in rats. *European Journal of Oncology*. 2005; 10(2):107-116.

Soffritti M, Padovani M, Tibaldi E, et al. Sucralose administered in feed, beginning prenatally through lifespan, induces hematopoetic neoplasias in male Swiss mice. *International Journal of Occupational and Environmental Health*. 2016; 22(1):7-17. [PubMed Abstract]

Chapter Four

Meal Prep Is Easy, Efficient, and Fun!

Due to busy days and activity-packed evenings, preparing meals ahead of time has become a mainstay in the lives of many families, including my own. Between swimming lessons, soccer games, and gymnastics practice, it's hard to carve out time to cook. What a treat it is to come home to a delicious, nourishing meal that takes me just minutes to get on the table! It's possible, with pre-planning and meal prepping.

The art of planning meals and preparing food a few days or a week before you eat it is a skill. Like all acquired skills, it takes practice! Shopping, chopping, cooking, baking, and properly storing and reheating meals, so they taste exceptionally great, takes some preparation. Even professional cooks and restaurant chefs tell me that they struggle with this very thing – preparing meals that go from refrigerator or freezer to the dining table in minutes. No surprise, really – this kind of cooking is a different animal than what happens in a professional culinary setting like a restaurant, where chefs pride themselves quickly converting fresh ingredients to menu items ready to be ordered. If they can learn to do it, so can you!

Over the years, I've gathered many tips and tricks to help this process run smoothly and efficiently. In this chapter, I hope to arm you with easy-to-follow suggestions and encouraging reassurance that you too can master the art of pre-planning and meal prepping. First, let me share with you one of the most common mistakes I see first-timers make: picking overly complicated recipes. While that Crispy Chicken with Tangy Sweet Sauce and Candied Walnuts may look and sound oh-so-delish, the many steps involved in the recipe are sure to slow you down, trip you up, and squash your confidence. Instead, when starting, select easy recipes with just a few necessary steps. Strive to ensure your family's first meal-prep experiences are enjoyable and stress free.

Before I go any further, let's start with why meal prepping is a lifesaver for busy families:

BENEFITS OF MEAL PREP

- **You'll save money.** While it may seem like common sense, you'll be surprised at how preparing your meals ahead of time will save you money. And right away too! Rather than spending $10–15 on lunch, you'll have a delicious meal that's healthy, quick, and ready to go, and costs a lot less! And, bonus – you can put that money towards that much-needed family vacation. Win-win!
- **You'll save time.** It might not feel like it at first, but the few hours you put in once per week will save you heaps of time overall. Investing a little time on the weekend, you'll find that your week runs more smoothly, you're more prepared, and you don't have to make as many decisions. Spending the time planning each week not only frees up your mental capacity for other things, it also means you'll have more time during the week to enjoy with family, time that you would typically have spent rushing to throw together a meal. Soon you'll come to recognize that meal prepping is the #1 way to find more quality time to spend with your family.
- **You'll waste less food.** With your meals planned out, you'll know what you're making and how much you need, so you will only buy the ingredients and amounts that you require. Sticking to a weekly menu also means that you'll stock your pantry with healthy food, helping you and your family eat better, feel better, and maintain a healthy weight.
- **You'll become more efficient when it counts most.** While it may not feel like it at first, you'll thank yourself for putting in a little elbow grease on the weekend to prepare for the week ahead.

When those busy evenings and late weeknights arrive, you'll pat yourself on the back for making a big batch of chili or grilled chicken and vegetables. It's so easy and satisfying to quickly warm up real food you've prepared, allowing you time to sit down, breathe, and enjoy a healthy meal with less stress. What a treat!

TIPS AND TRICKS FOR MEAL PREP SUCCESS

Knowledge and experience is the key to becoming skilled – I believe that to be true in almost everything, and it's certainly no different when it comes to meal prepping. Regardless of which recipes you select, if you can organize yourself and structure your meal prep time for maximal efficiency, you'll get more done and be happier about it! I'd love to share the pearls of wisdom I've collected over the years:

1 Invest in proper quality food storage containers

A crucial component of successful meal prepping is organizing yourself and your work environment. You'll need to quickly and easily access your ingredients, then store your prepared food properly to ensure it stays fresh and delicious.

Storage containers can make or break your meal prep experience. While cheap, plastic containers can leak, crack, and be a pain to store – either in your cupboard or in the fridge – good-quality containers will be easy to store and can be relied upon to keep your meals fresh.

I highly recommend going with glass containers, as they are the most eco-friendly and non-toxic option. Alternatively, if you're worried about your little ones breaking them, or if glass is simply too heavy, go for stainless steel containers or 100% pure food grade silicone. Avoid plastics, including BPA-free options, as all plastics contain harmful chemicals, whether they are labeled to indicate it or not. These components can leech into your food, especially if you're using the containers to heat up your meals or packing food into them while it is still hot. (Stop doing those things!)

When it comes to choosing what container sizes to purchase, limit yourself to just two or three sizes. This way you will be able to easily stack them in the fridge when full, fit them into each other when empty, and you won't need to go searching for lids when you're ready to use them.

2 Set aside 20–30 minutes each week to plan your menu

Create a physical or digital folder where you can store recipes that appeal to you and your family. Then each week, quickly flip through the folder and decide which meals you'd like to make that week. Watch for recipes that are easy to double or triple or ones that can be bulk-made and used several different ways for several different meals. For example, roasted vegetables make a great side dish for grilled chicken, fish, or veggie burgers, and they can be added to rice bowls, too.

3 Leave a little room for flexibility

Of course, being prepared is the name of the game, so is there such a thing as being overly prepared? No, not when it comes to meal prep. Preparation saves countless hours in the kitchen during your busy week.

While it's important to plan out your meals, there will be times when you have to make allowances for the unforeseen or unscheduled dinners at friends' houses or at a restaurant, or other events that may come up midweek. Don't be too rigid and plan every meal to a tee! You might find yourself having to throw out some of your pre-planned and carefully cooked meals, which is a real downer after all the time, energy, and expense you've put into them. Instead, allow for a bit of flexibility. You don't want to feel so tied to your schedule that you forgo some of the fun opportunities that come up at the last minute.

4 Variety is the spice of life

Arguably, nowhere is this statement more accurate than when it comes to meal prep. Almost nobody is okay with eating the same flavors over and over again. We get bored, and that spells disaster for sticking with a healthy eating routine. My favorite way to keep things interesting is to indulge in a wide variety of flavors, spices, and herbs.

Try making your sauces, condiments and salad dressings to keep on hand. Avoid using store-bought versions as these can be packed with preservatives, colorants, and sugar. Keep a varied spice rack, too, to offer new possibilities in your cooking. It's so easy to whip up a healthy salad dressing or sauce if you have the right ingredients and equipment in your stocked pantry.

I often hear friends and family say that they're nervous to try new spices or make recipes with flavors that they are unfamiliar with. I get it, but I'm here to help you break free of that fear! Take a look at my recipe for *Slow Cooker Tortilla Soup* (page 143). It's got several spices that I was unaccustomed to using. When I gathered up the courage to try them, the recipe quickly became one of my family's favorites.

5 Multi-tasking and batch cooking is king

A lot is going on in a dedicated meal-prep session! Ideally, you're making several recipes at once, which means you've got fingers in many pies. It is obvious why: there isn't enough time to make one recipe after another, start to finish. For highest efficiency, you'll need to work on several recipes (doubled or tripled) at the same time. This may feel overwhelming at first, but you'll get better and better at multi-tasking in the kitchen over time.

Tip: One-sheet or pot meals are best when it comes to multi-tasking, as they require very little ongoing attention. Try my *Roasted Vegetable Lasagna* (page 241) or *One-Pan Lemon Chicken Bake* (page 225). And if you're still not sure where to start, just follow my suggested meal-prep plan, below, to get you off on the right foot.

PRACTICAL WAYS TO GET YOUR KIDS INVOLVED IN MEAL PREP

Ever heard the saying, "Give your kid healthy food, they'll be healthy for a day. Teach them how to make healthy food, and they'll make healthy choices for a lifetime"? Getting your little ones involved in family meal prep comes with many benefits.

A study done by the University of Alberta took a look at the association between helping with meal prep at home and making healthy food choices in 3,398 fifth graders. The research revealed that the more often kids helped to prepare and cook meals at home, the more likely they were to select fruit, vegetables, and healthy foods when given a choice. The study concluded by saying that teaching children how to prepare healthy and straightforward meals could lead to an improvement in dietary habits.

Now, trust me, I hear you. With rambunctious four, eight-, and eleven-year-olds in my house, I know full well that pleasant little ones isn't always possible. However, I do my best to include them, knowing that getting them involved ensures that they will happily eat the food they've helped me prepare, preventing stressful mealtime meltdowns. Yay! Here are the strategies I use:

Focus on education and balance. I love to teach my kids about the nutrients they need for a healthy lifestyle and how to properly balance their meals. Planting these little seeds of knowledge in their brains means that they will be more mindful of the food decisions they make when I'm not around. When I pack their lunch and snacks, I always make sure to include fiber such as fruit and vegetables, healthy fats, and protein.

Let them make decisions. It's important for kids to feel that they're not just helping in the kitchen, they also have some authority over what is being prepared. Meal prep shouldn't be a chore for them. Instead, it should be something that they find fun. One way to include them in the decision-making is to have them help you pick the meals for the week. Sit them down with a recipe book or your meal-prep folder, and let them flip through. Once they choose a healthy recipe you can agree on, they'll be more enthusiastic about helping make it.

Delegate, delegate, delegate! If you have more than one child, delegating tasks can help speed up the process while also allowing them to take ownership of a certain aspect of the meal. Trust them with tasks such as getting ingredients from the cupboard, preparing and measuring the ingredients as is appropriate to their age, stirring the pot under your watch, and even cleaning up. When you involve your children, you'll need to be both ringmaster and team player to get everything done.

Let their creativity flow. Meal preparation doesn't have to follow a strict set of rules. Everything from the ingredients to the container choices is negotiable. If your children want to cut vegetables in a funky way, pick random containers (that are reasonably sized), or even add random ingredients that may work – be open to it! If they're enthusiastic about meal prep and contributing ideas, that means they're interested and engaged in the task. Shutting them down will only cause them to disengage and eventually see meal prep as an exhausting chore. Encourage them and everyone will have a lot more fun!

Plant an edible or herb garden. The awareness brought to children about where their food comes from has been proven to be a useful tool in getting them to eat more fruit and vegetables. You can plant seedlings to yield fresh fruit and vegetables, or, if space is limited, starting with an herb garden is a great option. Fresh herbs make an excellent addition to most recipes. Kids love peppermint!

HOW TO KEEP FOOD FRESH

With modern day refrigerators and cautious expiry dates, we've lost the ability to tell when food is safe to eat or when it's best to toss. For this reason, many people can be iffy when it comes to eating leftovers or prepping food several days before.

Additionally, if you're pregnant or feeding meals to children, it's important to take the proper precautions to eliminate as much chance of food contamination as possible. The safety tips below will help you avoid accidentally causing digestive upsets or promoting food-borne illnesses.

FOOD SAFETY TIPS

1. Once your food is prepared, be sure to cool it down as quickly as possible to room temperature. Don't let soups, stews, and casseroles sit out for hours to cool; instead transfer them to smaller, shallow containers, or place them in an ice bath to help cool quickly. Aim to have food cooled and in the fridge within 30 minutes for the safest standards.
2. Never put hot foods in the fridge or freezer as this will not only take a toll on your appliances, but could dangerously increase the temperature of other items, slightly warming and thawing them, and allowing bacteria to flourish.
3. If reheating foods from the fridge, be sure to heat to the original cooking temperature. This means that most cooked meals should be piping hot when re-served.
4. If thawing meals from the freezer, never leave them on the counter to soften. Thaw foods that come directly from the freezer in the oven or microwave, or allow them to thaw in the fridge for a day or so. Thawing food will enable bacteria to multiply and leaving foods at room temperature to defrost quickly allows for a much higher likelihood of bacteria growth – which can result in food poisoning.
5. Never refreeze foods that have been previously frozen without cooking them in between. As mentioned, when we thaw foods, the bacteria have a chance to multiply. If we then refreeze these foods without cooking them in between to kill the harmful bacteria, the second thawing could allow bacteria levels to become harmful. Cooking kills all the harmful bacteria. For example, it is okay to defrost ground beef, make a delicious Bolognese sauce and freeze this sauce, because the meat in the sauce was cooked before returning to the freezer.
6. When freezing foods to enjoy at a later date, freeze in reasonable portions for your family. It does not make sense to freeze huge portions, because you'll need to defrost the whole thing and refreeze what you don't eat, risking accidental bacterial contamination.

KARLENE'S STEP-BY-STEP MEAL PREP SCHEDULE (WITH SUGGESTED MEAL PLAN)

As you become more and more comfortable with meal prepping, you'll find your rhythm and groove. Over the years, I've discovered shortcuts to help me save time, and learned to clean up as I go, so I'm not left with a big mess at the end. I want to share with you what works for my family and me, in the hopes that you'll take away some useful tips and make them your own.

Book your meal prep time like an appointment

Busy schedules never end, and yes my family's calendar is no exception. Each day is jam-packed, whether it's the week or the weekend, which is why I book our meal-prep time each week as I would any other appointment. I know weekends can be hectic, so if we have a BBQ or a planned afternoon with loved ones, I always leave enough time in the earlier part of the day to prepare some meals. If we have a whole-day activity scheduled, I shift my meal prep to Saturday. Spending a couple of hours each weekend meal prepping is non-negotiable for me because I know it will keep my family healthy and help our week run more smoothly.

Scheduling a time during the weekend works best for me because I can prep the meals for the week ahead – feel free to pick any day that works with your schedule. Try to block at least three hours to give yourself enough time to prep, cook, package, and label and clean up. I like to grocery shop during the week, and visit a farmers' market or two on weekends to pick up fresh produce for snacks; however, if that doesn't work with your schedule, you can grocery shop all in one go, whenever it works best.

How to make grocery shopping less painful

Stick to your list. Grocery shopping can stretch out for what seems like countless hours, or it can be quick, efficient, and effortless. You can ensure it's the latter by strictly sticking to your grocery list; not buying items you don't need. There is only one reason I ever break this rule: items on sale, or fresh, local produce that I can easily substitute for something I have on my list. For example, if I have planned to have strawberries on hand for snacks, I will substitute raspberries if they have a good sale going on or if there is a big haul from local farmers. I also do this with greens like spinach and kale, or cruciferous vegetables such as broccoli and cauliflower.

About that list: it isn't something I jot down before I head out the door. Earlier, I've already spent 20–30 minutes organizing the meals I plan to make for the week, producing my list. I then carry it with me so I can make a big shopping trip when I find the time, or in shorter bursts throughout the week while waiting for the kids to finish an activity.

Shop early in the day. When it comes to grocery shopping, I recommend going as early as possible. I like to shop as close to the store opening hours as I can. This means that the shelves are well-stocked, I get the freshest produce, and I don't need to worry about negotiating around other people's carts. Farmers' markets are also another great place to pick up fresh fruit and vegetables when in season.

When I get home, I unpack my groceries. If I'm prepping right away, I leave non-perishable items on the counter, or if I don't plan to use them until later, I store them in easy-to-reach places. Remember always to store meat and dairy in the refrigerator until you're ready to use it.

Let's get prepping!

This is where strategy and experience come into play. I employ all the tips and tricks I have shared above to increase my efficiency and get everything I have planned done in a timely manner.

I start by looking at the week's recipes to determine where I can multitask. For example, can I do something else while the lasagna is baking in the oven? Or can I chop double the vegetables for both snacks and roasted sides?

I always try to start with the recipes that require a longer cooking time in the oven or on the stove. This way I can chop fresh vegetables or prepare no-bake energy balls while the meals are cooking and cooling. Another important question I ask myself: How can I prep two things at once so they can bake at the same time? Making full use of the oven's capacity isn't just efficient, it's energy efficient!

Don't forget the snacks! With energetic little ones in the house, easy grab-and-go snacks are crucial. Each week I make sure to focus on a couple of options. I chop an assortment of vegetables such as carrots, cucumber, celery, and cauliflower; setting them aside in a covered bowl or closed container of water in the fridge. This helps keep them crisp and fresh all week long, while also making it easy for the kids to dip in and grab whatever crunchy vegetables they want.

Pack, label, and store

Before I start a meal-prepping session, I always make sure to clear a shelf or section in my fridge. This way I'm not cramming the groceries and later the prepared meals into whatever little opening I can find. Making containers visible and easy to access means I can quickly and easily pack lunch-boxes; it also means that my family can quickly find and locate whatever they want.

Another great tip I learned from a fellow nutritionist years ago is to always test the size of your containers before packing them. Often, containers hold a lot more food than you would typically serve yourself on a regular-sized lunch or dinner plate. I suggest first plating the amount of food you'd normally consume, and then transferring it to the container. That's how you determine the size of the container you need for a regular-sized serving.

Of course, you won't need to check your containers every time you meal prep, but do it periodically. You may be surprised to see how hard it is to judge a reasonable serving size based on just eyeballing the container. We tend to be more familiar with what a regular portion looks like on a dinner plate than visualizing it in a container. Servings of food look much smaller in containers. If you pack a full container, you may be overeating or wasting food.

Once you've divided and packed away your meals for the week, be sure to label them clearly. You can either label each one with the date you prepared the meal, or you can label them by day of the week that you plan to enjoy them. Often a combination of both works best. That way you'll be organized for the week, and know how long your meals will last.

It may indeed feel like there is a lot to think about when you start meal prepping. By following the guidelines and tips above, you'll soon find your groove, and the dance will streamline and speed up. Just as it is with any skill, you'll get better and better with time, and your confidence will grow. Get your family involved and keep meal prep times short to keep it fun. Stay motivated. You'll be amazed at how much you can achieve in such a short time, plus you'll be passing on amazingly healthy eating habits to your children. You may think that meal prepping is something you're doing for your efficiency and sanity, nonetheless, your whole family will reap the benefits.

References

Chu YL1, Farmer A, Fung C, et al. Involvement in home meal preparation is associated with food preference and self-efficacy among Canadian children. *Public Health Nutr.* 2013; 16(1):108-12.

Suggested Meal Plan

To get you started on the right track, I've put together an easy-to-follow meal plan for the week. You can find all the delicious recipes in the recipe section. I've also included suggestions on where you can multitask to save you time, as well as suggestions on tasks that can involve the whole family.

Saturday/Sunday – write down your meal plan for the week. Make your grocery list and head to the store to do your big shop. **Sunday** – prep: energy balls, cashew dip, cut up vegetables, raspberry-chia jam, and overnight oats **Wednesday/Thursday** – quick stop at the store for a refresh on any perishable or needed items

MONDAY *("Meatless Monday")*

- **Breakfast** – Berry-banana oat smoothie
- **Lunch** – Avocado toast, fresh fruit
- **Snack** – Cut-up fresh vegetables, cashew dip
- **Dinner** – Cauliflower pasta with peas

TUESDAY

- **Breakfast** – 2 scrambled eggs, sprouted grain toast with raspberry-chia jam
- **Lunch** – Tuna wrap with collard greens
- **Snack** – *Snickers* energy balls
- **Dinner** – Coconut lentil, chickpea dhal with steamed basmati rice

WEDNESDAY

- **Breakfast** – Berry smoothie bowl
- **Lunch** – Leftover dhal
- **Snack** – Fresh vegetables with cashew dip
- **Dinner** – Roasted salmon with spinach chimichurri

THURSDAY

- **Breakfast** – Banana blender pancakes (make a double batch)
- **Lunch** – Cucumber noodle salad (you can prepare night before and add dressing just before serving)
- **Snack** – *Snickers* energy balls
- **Dinner** – One-pan lemon chicken drumsticks with vegetables

FRIDAY

- **Breakfast** – Banana blender pancakes (put in toaster to warm)
- **Lunch** – Leftovers from Thursday dinner
- **Snack** – Sliced apple with almond butter
- **Dinner** – Pizza night (I usually reserve one night a week for restaurant or takeout)

SATURDAY

- **Breakfast** – Vanilla pear and almond bake
- **Lunch** – Heirloom tomato soup
- **Dinner** – Curry lamb shank, basmati rice, green salad (many options to choose from; double the dressing to use for leftovers later in the week)

SUNDAY

- **Breakfast** – Lemon blueberry waffles (make double batch to have for Monday morning or freeze to use later in the week)
- **Lunch** – Leftover roasted tomato soup
- **Dinner** – Roasted vegetable lasagna, kale caesar salad, beet brownies

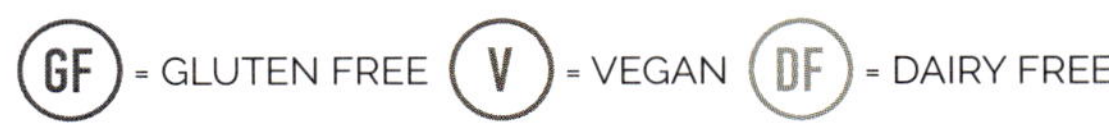

The Real Food Pantry

I present to you this chapter as a resource. I hope it will become well-thumbed as you use it not only to set up your pantry for smooth, efficient cooking, which is also nutritious. I also wish that this chapter becomes a resource that you refer back to it frequently for many years to come!

It may take a bit of time, however stocking your pantry to nourish your family is the single-best way to set yourself up for success. Buy the best-quality real food ingredients you can afford, and you will see, taste, and recognize the difference in how you feel.

Below I have outlined some of my favorite kitchen pantry staples. They are items you'll see come up time and time again in my recipes!

Flours

There is a wide assortment of flours available at the grocery store. While some of my recipes are made with whole wheat or spelt flour that contain gluten, I also love experimenting with gluten-free flours to add varieties of flavor, texture, and nutrients to our meals.

One of the most common questions I get asked is about substitutions. Gluten-free flours have particular properties and substituting them can take some experimentation. Coconut flour is very dry, while almond flour yields wetter baked goods. For the best results, I recommend following the recipes as I have outlined them. If you need to change it up due to dietary restrictions, be aware that you may need to play around with the qualities of each flour until you find the right blend.

Coconut Flour is merely dried and finely ground coconut meat. It is high in fiber, protein, and healthy fats and makes a great grain-free and nut-free flour option. It helps maintain healthy blood sugar levels and supports digestive health; a little goes a long way, so measure carefully (if making a substitution for all-purpose flour, you may only need ¼–⅓ the amount, plus double the eggs). A small amount short or extra can change the entire consistency of a recipe. Store coconut flour in an airtight container in the fridge for up to six months and the freezer for up to 12 months. The flour should smell sweet and nutty. If it has a bitter taste, it has gone bad and should be discarded.

Almond Flour has a naturally sweet taste making it a great gluten-free option for delicious baked goods such as cakes, cookies, and muffins. It is made from blanched (skinned) almonds. The finer the grind, the better your baked goods will turn out. If the flour is coarsely ground, your baked goods may come out overly moist and gritty. Coarsely ground almond flour is commonly sold at grocery stores, so for best results, see my resource guide for the brands I recommend. When storing almond flour, keep enough for 1–2 weeks of baking in an airtight container in your pantry. Store the rest in an airtight container in the fridge for up to six months and the freezer for up to 12 months. If it has a bitter taste, it has gone bad and should be discarded.

Almond Meal. Not to be confused with almond flour, almond meal is coarser, and the skins are typically not removed. It works very well as a bread-crumb substitute on breaded fish and chicken, but not as well in baked goods. You can easily make your own at home by pulsing raw almonds in a food processor, be sure not to overblend or you will end up with almond butter.

Sprouted Spelt Flour is an alternative to whole wheat flour in recipes. While it contains gluten, it seems to be better tolerated by those with sensitivities due in part to the sprouting process. Sprouting makes nutrients more readily available and more natural to absorb and digest. It also allows for spelt's unique nutty flavor to come through, creating delicious baked goods such as bread, muffins, cookies, and crackers. Store opened flour in the fridge or freezer to keep fresh.

Whole Wheat Flour is rich in fiber and an excellent alternative to white, processed flour. The whole grain is milled including the bran, the germ, and the endosperm, meaning much of the nutrient content stays intact. Since the bran and the germ are high in nutrients and oils, they are more prone to spoiling and can go rancid quickly. They also make a tastier snack for many common pantry pests, so whole grain flours have a relatively short shelf life of just a few months. It's best to keep your flour in the freezer, either in a Mason jar or a large Ziploc bag, to prevent it from going rancid or getting bug-infested. If you don't have freezer space, the fridge is okay, as it will slow down the degeneration.

Oat Flour is created by grinding whole oats. You can easily make it at home by grinding oats in a high-speed blender or coffee/spice grinder. It is a great gluten-free option, having a consistency similar to wheat flour when used in pancakes and baked goods. Use it for its sweet, nutty flavor and its excellent ability to become gelatinous and bind together, which is perfect for use in vegan or egg-free recipes. Oat flour has many health benefits including helping to lower the risk of heart disease, reducing cholesterol levels, and stabilizing blood sugar. Thanks to its high-fat content, oat flour spoils quickly. Store unused flour in the refrigerator or freezer. Bring it to room temperature before using.

Rice Flour is an excellent allergen-free option. It works well as a thickener for soups and sauces; and while not as nutrient-dense as some of the other flours, it is a helpful option for those trying to uncover food sensitivities because it rarely causes allergic reactions. It is high in fiber and contains choline, a nutrient crucial in helping to maintain healthy liver function. Brown rice flour has the husk included, providing extra nutrients.

Buckwheat Flour is made from ground buckwheat kernels. While "wheat" is in the name, it is, in fact, gluten and wheat free. This is because buckwheat is not a grain, but a seed. It is rich in fiber, protein, and nutrients such as magnesium and B vitamins. Buckwheat flour is used in pancakes, scones, muffins, and bread; it has a bold, earthy flavor that can take some getting used to. It also has a moist and tender texture in small amounts and can be chalky in larger quantities, so it is better combined with other flours.

Alternatives to Sugar

Coconut Sugar is made by dehydrating the liquid sap from the flower buds of the coconut tree. Coconut sugar, also known as palm sugar, is what remains once the water is evaporated from the coconut nectar. It is similar to brown sugar in taste and color; and can be substituted for maple syrup in equal quantities, resulting in less sweetness and deeper amber color.

Coconut Nectar is the sap from the flower buds of the coconut tree. It contains a wide variety of nutrients including vitamin C, B vitamins, and amino acids. While not a widely used sugar alternative, it can be found in some health food stores and offers an opportunity to add variety to recipes.

Maple Syrup is one of my favorite sweeteners. It is a great natural, unrefined liquid sweetener that enhances the flavor of dishes by adding sweetness and depth of flavor. Canada produces 71% of the world's maple syrup, making this an excellent way to support countries who are creating pure, unrefined sweeteners.

Raw Honey is one of nature's true superfoods with a ton of health benefits. It provides energy, boosts the immune system, and can help with seasonal allergies. When purchasing honey, opt for a reputable supplier, like a local farmer at a farmers' market, to ensure you are getting the best-quality product and that the hive and bees are treated humanely.

Applesauce is a great sugar substitute in baked goods. To replace sugar in recipes with applesauce, merely reduce the liquid content. It adds moisture, nutrients, and lots of fiber. When purchasing store-bought, opt for organic and unsweetened. You can also easily make your own by coring, peeling, slicing, and steaming apples until soft. Then, using an immersion or high-speed blender, puree until smooth.

Dates are the fruit of the date palm tree which closely resembles a coconut palm tree. Most fruits get their weight from water, however up to 70% of a date's weight comes from its own sugar. Yet, even though they are naturally sweet, they are an excellent source of fiber, and high in beta-glucans which help promote normal blood glucose levels. Dates are also very rich in potassium.

Dried Fruits such as dates, raisins, figs, and prunes make excellent substitutes for eggs and honey in baked foods. They can be pulsed in a food processor to create a paste which can be added in smoothies, brownies, energy balls, pasta sauce, homemade ketchup, salad dressings, and more. Make sure to buy organic and sulfite-free dried fruits. Sulfites are used as preservatives, and while they generally do not cause a problem, in some people, they can cause headaches, asthma attacks, and other allergy-like symptoms. While they naturally occur in some foods, minimizing your exposure will help reduce the chances of suffering an allergy attack or developing an allergy.

Super Grains

Quinoa is an ancient grain first grown and consumed by the Incas almost four thousand years ago. It is rich in protein with 14 g of protein per 100 g of quinoa. It is also gluten-free, high in fiber and packs nutrients like iron, magnesium, and B2. It is an excellent alternative to rice and other grains; and can be used as a side dish, in salads, as a breakfast porridge option, or as a base for chili and stir-fries. It can also be added to soups and used to make meat-free burgers. An excellent high-protein choice for vegans and vegetarians, quinoa can also be ground into a flour for use in baked goods, waffles, and pancakes.

Buckwheat is a seed, not a grain, making it naturally free of gluten. It has a bold nutty, earthy flavor and seedy bite. Take note of the difference between raw buckwheat groats and toasted buckwheat, also known as kasha. When cooked, groats keep their shape, much like rice, while kasha turns to a porridge consistency and is an excellent alternative to oatmeal for a protein- and nutrient-rich breakfast.

Rolled Oats are naturally gluten and wheat free. However, they are processed in facilities that also handle wheat and gluten-containing grains. If you wish to avoid gluten in your oats be sure to purchase brands that are certified gluten-free oats. The fiber in oats helps lower the risk of heart disease, reduce cholesterol levels, stabilize blood sugar, and promote healthy bowel movements. Oats can be processed in many ways including steel-cut, rolled, and instant. Processing affects cooking time and how best to use the oats. Rolled oats are lightly steamed to soften the groats and make them pliable; the groats are then flattened. This means that they hold their shape better and are best used for breakfast cereals, granola bars, cookies, muffins, and other baked goods. Once opened, store rolled oats in an airtight container to protect them from bug infestations and rancidity.

Flavor and Nutrient Boosters

Cacao Nibs are a delicious sugar-free alternative to chocolate chips. They are merely the crushed bits of a raw cacao bean, which are high in antioxidants and nutrients such as iron, magnesium, and fiber. They add a great crunch to smoothies, breakfast cereals, baked goods, and homemade trail mix. Chocolatey in taste though a bit bitter, they are chocolate in its purest form, and they have a texture similar to roasted coffee beans. You can find cacao nibs in the health food or organic baking section of your grocery store. Keep cacao nibs away from direct sunlight and store in an airtight bag, and the nibs will stay fresh for two to three years.

Cacao Powder is made by grinding raw cocoa beans and extracting the fat (cacao butter). The process keeps the living enzymes, antioxidants, and nutrients in the resulting cacao powder intact, making it a superior product to cocoa powder. In contrast, cocoa powder is raw cacao powder that has been roasted at high temperatures, removing many of the nutrients, antioxidants, and health benefits. For maximum nutrition, I like to use cacao powder to add rich, chocolatey flavor to smoothies, cookies, cakes, and other baked goods.

Dark Chocolate Chips are the ultimate comfort and superfood. Just like regular chocolate chips, the dark variety adds a delicious chocolatey flavor to baked goods, breakfasts, and more. I prefer dark chips as they are lower in sugar and contain more significant health benefits. Before purchasing chocolate chips, be sure to check the ingredients list and avoid buying chips with any additives or thickeners like soy lecithin and artificial flavors. My favorite brand is *Enjoy Life* as their chips are vegan and additive free, as well as soy and dairy free.

Matcha Powder is also known as green tea powder. It is packed with nutrients and antioxidants; and while it does contain caffeine, it is balanced with L-theanine, an amino acid that promotes relaxation and restful sleep while calming the nervous system and relieving symptoms of anxiety. Matcha provides an even boost of energy, especially compared to coffee. Many people crave a warm, energizing morning drink, so rather than quitting coffee cold turkey, try substituting it with a creamy, frothy matcha latte. In direct contrast to coffee, matcha helps regulate blood sugar levels, controlling insulin and promoting an anti-inflammatory response. It also helps reduce the risk of heart disease, fights aging, supports healthy liver detoxification and prevents diabetes. When purchasing matcha, be sure to choose a good-quality, unsweetened, organic product. Unfortunately, many of the green tea products on the market are high in heavy metals, especially lead. When green tea is steeped, the heavy metals remain in the leaf, however, since matcha powder contains the whole ground leaf, it is particularly important to select a quality product to avoid heavy metal contamination.

Whey Protein Powder. Whey is a type of protein derived from dairy, making it a good option for those who don't have trouble digesting dairy. Whey is easy to absorb and can help boost your immune system. It also generally tastes the best of all the protein powders. However, it's important to make sure that you are not experiencing any symptoms like gas, bloating, skin rashes, and breakouts, when consuming whey-based powders. When selecting a whey protein powder, choose an isolate which has high levels of protein, opt for cross-flow filtration system as the method of extraction (it should say this on the tub of a good-quality protein powder), and look for New Zealand whey. Whey extracted from New Zealand dairy is the healthiest option as all cows are grass-fed and the New Zealand government mandates that all dairy products be free of chemical residue, hormones, and antibiotics.

Vegan Blend Protein Powder is also called plant-based protein powder. When selecting this protein option, I always opt for a blend because it ensures that I get a variety of protein types, thus avoiding possible sensitivities, and resulting in a more balanced nutrient ratio. Plant proteins, compared to animal proteins, are often considered incomplete, meaning that they do not contain all the essential amino acids. By using a blended plant-based protein powder, we can balance out the amino acids, making for a complete protein blend. Popular choices include brown rice, hemp, and pea. I recommend avoiding protein powders that contain additives such as maltodextrin, soy, or artificial sweeteners, and flavors.

Fermented Protein & Greens is an excellent upgrade to protein powder. Adding greens adds tons of nutrients while fermenting helps predigest those nutrients, making them easier to absorb by our bodies and thus increasing the amount we can consume. Fermenting also adds good probiotics to the powder, helping to boost our immune system and promote digestive health, while removing any "anti-nutrients" that can hinder nutrient absorption. When it comes to taste and gastrointestinal tolerance, fermented powders are one of the best choices.

Healthy Fats

After much debate throughout the decades, we now know that healthy fats are an essential and beneficial part of a nourishing diet. Indeed, studies show that when we include healthy fats in our diet, we not only enjoy the benefits of the nutrients in the fats, we also enhance our absorption of nutrients elsewhere in the meal. One study published in the

Journal of Nutrition found that adding avocado oil resulted in a multiple-fold increase of the absorption of nutrients from a salad. Not only are healthy fats nutritious on their own, but they also help make other nutrients more bioavailable and easy to absorb. Another reason why I love adding healthy fats to my family's diet is because they are so good at helping to reduce symptoms of inflammation, which can lead to a variety of diseases namely inflammatory bowel diseases such as Crohn's and Colitis; skin disorders such as acne, eczema, and psoriasis; allergies, asthma, and autoimmune diseases such as arthritis, and more. Healthy fats are also an excellent source of energy as they help fuel our bodies and brains.

Coconut Oil is one of the healthiest of the cooking oils commonly used today. It is easy to digest and contains many medicinal benefits, thanks to its antimicrobial and antibacterial properties. It is made up of medium-chain triglycerides (MCTs) which, rather than being stored as fat, are used by our bodies as quick fuel. It's, therefore, a great source of energy. It's also excellent for high-heat cooking and, because it's slow to oxidize and go stale, it's a great kitchen staple.

Ghee or clarified butter is butter that has had the milk solids almost entirely removed. This process leaves behind only the healthy, buttery fat, and makes ghee an excellent choice for those that have trouble digesting lactose and casein. It has a high-smoke point and can be used for frying, sautéing, and roasting. Ghee can be easily prepared at home or purchased ready-made. If opting for store-bought varieties, always select organic and grass-fed ghee for maximum nutrients.

Avocado Oil is an excellent choice for both cold preparations and, due to its high-smoke point and high-heat cooking. It has an assortment of health benefits including promoting heart and skin health. It is also high in lutein, a vital nutrient for good eyesight. When selecting avocado oil, opt for cold pressed to get the most benefits. I like to drizzle a little avocado oil into my smoothies and on salads or use it in marinades when grilling meat. It also works well in baked goods, when roasting vegetables, and in homemade mayonnaise and sauces. It has a mild flavor that lends well too many dishes.

Grapeseed Oil is a byproduct of winemaking, produced from the grape seeds left behind after wine is made by pressing the grapes. The health benefits of grapeseed oil are controversial due mainly to how the oil is processed. Most commercially available grapeseed oil is produced using chemical solvents such as hexane, a known air pollutant and neurotoxin. Also, during processing, grapeseed oil may also be heated to very high temperatures that can oxidize the oil and make it go rancid. For this reason, it's crucial to purchase grapeseed oil that has been cold pressed or expeller pressed as these processes do not use chemical solvents or high heat during processing. When cold pressed, grapeseed oil is an excellent source of vitamin E, an important antioxidant that helps protect cells from the damaging free radicals associated with cancer, heart disease, and dementia. It has a neutral flavor and works well with many recipes.

Extra Virgin Olive Oil is an excellent choice for low-heat sautéing, cold salads, and other cold dishes. To ensure the best product, purchase cold-pressed oil that is packaged in dark, glass bottles, as EVOO is heat and light sensitive. Additionally, always read the ingredient label, as many companies mix in lower-quality oils and not all products are 100% pure extra virgin olive oil. Store the oil in a cool place. When cooking with EVOO, heat oil gradually and add a little bit of water when sautéing vegetables – if you are not using high-water content vegetables like zucchinis or peppers. This way there is less chance for the oil to reach its smoke point and oxidize.

Walnut Oil has a rich, nutty flavor that is perfect for salad dressings, grilled meat, and fish dishes, and drizzled over freshly cooked pasta. It is best used cold or at room temperature as it can become bitter when heated. When purchasing walnut oil, opt for unrefined, cold-pressed oil to ensure maximum health benefits. Walnut oil is rich in phytonutrients and is an excellent source of minerals (e.g., magnesium, zinc, iron, and calcium). It's also packed with B vitamins, and antioxidants namely selenium and vitamin E. Walnut oil has a shelf life of six months, which can be extended by storing it in the fridge.

Pumpkin Seed Oil is an excellent choice to add extra nutrients, health benefits, and flavor variety to cold dishes such as salads and smoothies. Pumpkin seed oil should be cold pressed and raw, as heat destroys many of the health benefits and makes the oil taste bitter. It is essential to store the oil properly to prevent it from going rancid. Always purchase oil in a dark bottle and store in a cool, dark place or the fridge. As pumpkin seed oil can turn rancid so quickly, it's a good idea to wipe away any stray drops on the bottle after using so that they don't contaminate the rest of the oil. Pumpkin seed oil helps reduce inflammation, promotes mental well-being, fights hair loss in males and has many anti-cancer properties. If the flavor of the oil is too strong for you, it works well combined with another mild-flavored oil.

Flaxseed Oil is an excellent, plant-based source of omega-3 fatty acids. Flaxseed oil is used cold in salads, smoothies, and dips. Flaxseed oil promotes weight loss, relieves constipation, reduces eczema, and other inflammatory conditions, as well as boosts heart health and the immune system. Flaxseed oil should be kept in the fridge, consumed raw and cold pressed, and never heated.

Vinegars

Just like good wine, investing in good-quality vinegar will go a long way in making your finished dishes taste great. Fortunately, when it comes to vinegar, a little goes a long way, so purchase the best quality you can afford. Store your vinegar in a dry cupboard, and they will last almost indefinitely. In fact, most will continue to mature and become better with age.

Apple Cider Vinegar (ACV) is one of my favorite pantry staples because it's packed with so many health benefits. To take full advantage, select a raw, unpasteurized product with the mother included. This way all the healthy bacteria and nutrients are still intact and can be used in the body. ACV is made from fermented apples. It can be, added to salads, taken as a shot, or taken in diluted water first thing in the morning to get the digestion moving. It promotes detoxification in the body, aids weight loss, assists lymphatic drainage, and helps balance gut bacteria. AVC is a superfood.

Balsamic Vinegar should be dark brown and syrupy. It has a smooth, sweet-and-sour flavor which makes it an excellent choice for creamy salad dressings, marinades, roasted vegetables, stews, and sauces. It is made from reduced grape juice that is aged in wooden casks; the best-quality, balsamic vinegar is aged for over 100 years. Like excellent wine, these vinegars can be very expensive. More typically balsamic vinegar sold at stores are aged for three to four years. While even these can be slightly pricey, it is worth investing in true balsamic vinegar, since it only takes a little to elevate your dishes.

Red Wine Vinegar is made by naturally fermenting red wine. The color can vary from pale pink to maroon depending on the wine used. Good-quality red wine vinegar is tangy and has a well-rounded taste. Quality red wine vinegar is aged for several months in wooden barrels, while cheaper varieties have a sharp, sour taste because they are produced quickly by brewing red wine with vinegar-soaked Beachwood shavings. I like to use red wine vinegar in salad dressings, marinades, and pickles. I also choose it for dishes that require vinegar and contain red cabbage or red meat, as the vinegar enhances these flavors.

White Wine Vinegar is made by naturally fermenting white wine for several months in wooden barrels. In quality products, this produces a mellow, rounded taste with aromatic flavors. Some cheaper versions are fermented quickly, resulting in a sharp, tart taste that may cause poorer results than the more expensive varieties. Since I enjoy using this vinegar in salads, sauces, dips, and marinades, I make sure to invest in a good-quality brand.

Regular White Vinegar. I use regular white vinegar to wash fruits and vegetables, which is especially important when not buying organic produce. White vinegar is also a great natural option for housecleaning and laundry. It can also be used as a cheap pickling vinegar; however, when using vinegar in my recipes, I always prefer to use a pure, naturally fermented vinegar that adds more nutritional value and aromatic flavor when compared to the regular kind.

Beans and Legumes

Black Beans are an excellent source of protein, fiber, and vital nutrients such as folate and copper. Their rich and creamy texture means they are the perfect choice for soups, stews, chili, or as a filling for wraps. Black beans are one of my go-to options for a quick, easy, and hearty dish for my family. When purchasing precooked, canned beans, be sure to select an organic product packaged in a BPA-free can.

Lentils are so versatile, cheap and delicious. They come in an assortment of varieties including green, red, and brown lentils. They are an excellent source of fiber and protein and cook up quickly. I like to use dried lentils to thicken soups, make hearty Indian-inspired dishes, or add to hot and cold salads. They also make an excellent side dish option for fish and chicken dishes. Some varieties hold their shape better than others, so it's essential to choose the right lentil for your recipe. Store dry lentils in a cool, dry pantry in an airtight container for up to one year.

Chickpeas have garnered much popularity for their creamy, delicious texture and flavor. They are an excellent source of fiber and protein, and a great option to add to salads, soups, stews, and dips like hummus. For ease of use, I recommend buying them precooked in a BPA-free can or glass jar. If you decide to purchase dry chickpeas, they will need to be soaked for a few hours before cooking. Any leftover cooked chickpeas can be frozen for use at a later date.

Pasta

Whole Grain Pasta includes all three layers of the wheat kernel: the bran, the germ, and the endosperm. Since the entire kernel is used, whole grain pasta contains more nutrients like iron and B vitamins compared to white pasta. Also, because of its higher fiber content, whole grain pasta is an excellent choice for reducing blood sugar levels and keeping you feeling fuller for longer, especially when paired with healthy fats and protein, as in roasted vegetables or a delicious Bolognese sauce.

Gluten-free Pasta. In recent years, a variety of delicious and healthful gluten-free pasta options have become widely available. Made with ingredients like red or green lentils, chickpeas, yellow and green peas, sweet potatoes and more, they offer a nutritious alternative to the typical rice- and corn-based gluten-free pasta options. As most diets are already high in rice and corn, I like to opt for the other superfood alternatives. It may take a little time to test different brands, and play around with cooking times, to get the best pasta consistency. However, I like to mix it up and add a variety of nutrients while still enjoying the hearty pasta texture and taste.

Salts, Spices, and Flavorings

Sea Salt. By purchasing a pure, quality sea salt, you'll enjoy all the health benefits sea salt has to offer, without any of the adverse effects of salt that we commonly hear about in the media. Sea salt is rich in trace minerals and an excellent source of electrolytes. It also helps prevent dehydration and balances fluid in the body, promotes a healthy immune system, improves brain function, eliminates mucous buildup, and alkalizes the body. It also prevents muscle cramps, encourages proper nerve function, increases energy, promotes heart health, and regulates sleep. There are several different kinds of sea salt, including pink Himalayan salt and Celtic sea salt.

Pink Himalayan Salt is far superior to regular table salt, which consists almost exclusively of sodium. In contrast, pink Himalayan contains dozens of trace minerals and elements, including magnesium, potassium, calcium, copper, and iron. Rather than raising blood pressure, pink salt can help regulate many processes in the body, including reducing blood pressure and pH as well as acting as a digestive aid and assisting in replenishing essential minerals lost through sweating and other body processes. These minerals also help reduce leg cramps, provide circulatory system support, and improve bone strength, and much more. With the rise in popularity of pink salt, some companies deceivingly dye regular salt to charge a premium, so be sure to purchase your Himalayan salt from a reputable company.

Pepper or ground peppercorns are available in several varieties. I prefer using black or white pepper in my recipes to not only add its flavor, but to also enhance the characteristics of the other ingredients. When it comes to getting the best flavor, freshly ground is best. Preground and cracked pepper will eventually go stale, so I recommend purchasing fresh, whole peppercorns and investing in a pepper grinder. Pepper's flavor diminishes during cooking, so season dishes towards the end of cooking or at the table for the best taste.

Nutritional Yeast is one of my favorite flavorings because it's not only delicious, it is also so good for you. It adds a naturally savory, cheesy, nutty flavor to dishes without the need for dairy. It's also rich in protein and crucial nutrients such as B vitamins for energy and mood balancing, as well as chromium for blood sugar regulation. Nutritional yeast is a deactivated form of yeast that has been pasteurized, so it does not contribute to any yeast overgrowths in the body, like candida. It makes a healthy vegan and dairy-free alternative in cheese sauces, Caesar salad dressing, and to sprinkle on veggie chili or crispy kale chips. You can find nutritional yeast in bags, often in the fridge, or in the bulk section of grocery stores. It can be stored for up to a year in a sealed bag in a cool, dry place, in the fridge, or for up to two years in a sealed bag in the freezer.

Oregano is a must-have spice rack essential. It adds delicious flavor to all sorts of dishes from lamb to vegetables, stuffings, egg dishes, and pasta sauces. I also like to add fresh oregano to salad dressings. It loses its potency quickly, so be sure to buy it in small batches to use it up immediately, and store it in a cool, dry cupboard. Also, oregano oil is one of the most potent natural antibacterial oils. It is often used to prevent and treat upper respiratory tract illnesses, gastrointestinal infections like parasites, menstrual cramps, and urinary tract infections. When consumed, fresh and dried oregano provide antioxidants to boost the immune system, and anti-inflammatory and antimicrobial properties to prevent coughs, colds, and flu.

Thyme is another kitchen essential. There are many different varieties, both cultivated and wild, with an array of flavors including mint, caraway, lemon, and stronger varieties that taste more like oregano. Thyme is best when fresh; you can also buy it freeze-dried. I like to use it in most meat dishes, including chicken, lamb, and fish, as well as roasted vegetables. Its strong flavor pairs well with rosemary and lemon, and means that it holds up well with long cooking times, making it a great addition to slow-cooked stews.

Rosemary is a staple in our kitchen, thanks in part to my Italian husband. This favorite Mediterranean herb compliments a wide variety of dishes, including roasted vegetables, rich meats like lamb, soups, stews, and casseroles. Rosemary is not only fragrant and delicious, it's also so good for you. It has unique compounds including Rosmarinic acid and essential oils which provide amazing anti-inflammatory, anti-fungal, anti-bacterial, and antiseptic properties.

Garlic Powder is made by dehydrating and grinding fresh garlic. It contains many health benefits including strong antibacterial and immune-boosting properties. When dried, garlic's flavor becomes more subtle and is an excellent ingredient in soups, stews, salad dressing, and sauces. Dried garlic retains its flavor well when stored in an airtight container, in a cool, dry place; and can last for many months and even years.

Mustard. So often I see people shy away from adding mustard, worrying that its intense flavor will overpower their recipes. With so many varieties of mustard, you can find just the right one to add a little kick of flavor without overwhelming the dish. Yellow, brown, or black mustard seeds yield dried mustard, Dijon mustard, whole grain mustard, yellow mustard, and so many more. Yellow mustard seeds are the mildest, and I love using dried mustard powder or Dijon mustard in many of my dishes.

Red Pepper Flakes are spicy flakes made from cayenne-type peppers. Also known as crushed red pepper, they add a delicious, spicy kick to pasta sauce, stews, sausages, and more; and are often provided as a condiment for dishes at Mediterranean restaurants. Since each product can vary in spice level depending on the exact peppers used, I recommend adding a little and adjusting after tasting, especially if you're sensitive to spicy food or cooking for younger children.

Tamari is made by fermenting soy beans, and it is similar to soy sauce in flavor. In contrast to soy sauce, however, it contains no wheat or gluten, making it an excellent option for those with sensitivities. Tamari has a salty, rich flavor, and works well in marinades, stir-fries, sauces, dips, and dressings. As it's made with soy beans, I always make sure to purchase an organic option to avoid genetically modified soy. Nowadays, tamari can easily be found in most grocery stores in the Asian section or the health food section.

THE REAL FOOD FRIDGE

Nuts, Seeds, and Butters

Cashews have a deliciously creamy, fatty texture and mild flavor. They are incredibly versatile and can be used in both savory dishes like stir-fries and also in sweet desserts. They're an excellent dairy replacement in vegan cheesecakes and creamy sauces. When soaked and blended with water, cashews also make a wonderful non-dairy milk alternative that's slightly sweet, creamy and, unlike other nut milk, is ready to drink without straining. Cashew butter is something we commonly use in my house to provide flavor and variety to our healthy fat intake. I love adding cashew butter to smoothies, drizzling it over breakfast foods like pancakes and waffles, or just enjoying a spoonful as a quick and nutritious snack. Roasted cashews also make a hearty, filling snack on their own or a great addition to granola.

Almonds are packed with nutrients like vitamin E, B2 (riboflavin) and magnesium, along with fiber, protein, and healthy fats. Almonds can help lower cholesterol and prevent heart disease and heart attacks; their high healthy fat content keeps you feeling fuller longer. They also support proper brain function, maintain glowing skin, control blood sugar levels, fight inflammation and improve digestive health. When soaked, peeled and blended with water, they make a tremendous non-dairy milk alternative. Whole almonds are an excellent snack and can be added to breakfast cereals and granola. I also love to use almond butter on toast with jam or toasted almonds for added crunch on salads.

Peanuts. While commonly mistaken for nuts, peanuts are, in fact, a member of the pea family. They grow in pods under the ground, and for this reason, they can contain high levels of a specific fungi which produces a group of toxins called aflatoxin. To ensure that you're not ingesting any aflatoxins, I always recommend purchasing organic peanut butter. It's important to always eat a variety of foods, so try mixing it up with other nut and seed butters for maximum nutrition.

Sesame Seeds are incredibly high in calcium, making them a great food for strong bones and teeth. They are also high in iron and magnesium and help the liver in detoxification. Whole sesame seeds can be sprinkled onto baked goods and salads; while sesame oil is a great option for sauces, salad dressings, and dips, as well as being an excellent high-heat cooking oil for stir-fries. Ground sesame seeds are used to make tahini, a smooth paste commonly added to Middle Eastern dishes.

Tahini, also known as sesame seed paste, is a thick paste made from ground sesame seeds. Tahini is most commonly used in Middle Eastern dishes like hummus and baba ganoush, a dip made from roasted eggplants. Tahini is a great option to add to sauces and dips to give them a luscious, creamy texture, and it also contributes to desserts.

Hemp Seeds have recently exploded in popularity, and not just in health food circles. These small seeds are packed full of healthy fats and can be toasted or eaten raw. They have a mild, nutty flavor that works well when sprinkled on salads, soups, and oatmeal, or blended into smoothies. Hemp seeds help fight inflammation and are a rich source of magnesium, which is key in reducing muscle cramps. They also help combat menopausal and PMS symptoms. Hemp seeds can be used to make hemp milk, hemp protein powder, and hemp oil.

Chia Seeds are tiny black or white seeds. They are full of nutrients including fiber, protein, antioxidants, calcium, magnesium, and omega 3s. They're great for skin health, digestive health, and heart health. When added to liquid they form a jelly-like substance which can mimic eggs in vegan recipes; it can also be used to make deliciously creamy chia pudding or added to smoothies and other sauces for thickening.

Flaxseeds are small brown, tan, or golden-colored seeds containing lots of nutrients such as fiber, protein, and omega-3s. They are excellent for healthy skin and hair, reducing cholesterol and promoting healthy bowel movements. When mixed with water, they create a gelatinous mass that can be substituted for eggs in baking. They are best absorbed when ground, however, due to their high-fatty acid content, they are prone to rancidity. I recommend grinding them fresh at home in a coffee grinder, or storing ground flaxseeds in the freezer. They should be slightly sweet and nutty. If they taste bitter, they have gone rancid and should not be used.

Pumpkin Seeds, also known as pepitas, can be eaten raw or roasted, and are used in both sweet and savory dishes. They are rich in protein, magnesium, iron, and zinc, helping to boost the immune system as well as promote muscle relaxation and support prostate health in men. They make a fantastic addition to salads, soups, as a stand-alone snack, or in protein balls. They are also high in the amino acid, tryptophan, which promotes restful sleep. Pumpkin seed oil and pumpkin seed butter are even great options to add to your diet.

Sunflower Seeds are one of the most common seeds in North America. They are a delicious and healthy snack and can be added to foods like salads, breakfast cereals and granolas, soups, protein balls, and smoothie bowls. Sunflower seeds are very high in antioxidants, namely vitamin E and selenium, which help reduce inflammation, promote heart health, lower cholesterol levels, support healthy thyroid function and promote skin health. I also like to have sunflower seed butter on hand as it makes a tasty alternative to peanut butter.

Walnuts are arguably one of the healthiest nuts available. These tiny brain-shaped morsels are excellent for brain health. Thanks to their high-healthy fat content, they are also suitable for heart health, reducing inflammation and increasing male fertility. They are a rich source of B vitamins, which help boost mood and energy levels. I love using walnuts to add texture and crunch to salads. Due to their high-omega-3 oil content, they can go rancid quickly, so store them in a cool, dark place, and use as soon as possible. The fridge will prolong their shelf life, as will purchasing walnuts in the shell.

Meat, Eggs, Dairy, and Non-Dairy Alternatives

Chicken. When selecting chicken and poultry, I recommend buying the best quality you can afford. An organic label on poultry ensures that the animals have been fed organic feed, and contain no hormones or antibiotics. It does not, however, guarantee the animals' living conditions. They may be kept in cages, and they may not have enjoyed any access to the outdoors during their lives. The best option for poultry is pasture raised. This label ensures that the animals receive ample opportunity and space to roam around outside, often on organically managed pastures.

Beef. When selecting beef be sure to purchase meat that is both hormone and antibiotic free. For the highest standard and maximum nutrients, purchase grass-fed beef, but be aware that the term "Grass-fed" is not regulated. While it often means exactly what you imagine, that the cattle have happily grazed in a pasture their whole lives, it could also mean other things. For example, it could mean "they ate grass until we started feeding them grain to fatten them up for market." It could also mean "we raised them on grain but let them graze for a few weeks so we could say they were grass-fed." A cow that has been sustained on mother's milk, fresh grass, and grass-type hay contains the highest levels of antioxidants, beta-carotene, and vitamin D; as well as 2–3 times healthier omega-3s as conventional grain fed beef. My advice: Get to know your butcher! Ask questions. Your butcher will know all about the beef that will be bought for your local market.

Salmon. When selecting salmon, halibut and other fish, I recommend always opting for a wild, sustainably caught product. Commercial fishing ventures worldwide net up to 40% by-catch, including dolphins, sea turtles, whales, seabirds, and other marine life. Often these animals are injured or even killed in the process. By selecting sustainably caught, hook-and-line seafood, we can significantly reduce the number of animals unnecessary harmed in the fishing process. Also, wild-caught fish contain higher levels of omega-3s and vitamin D, compared to factory-farmed fish that are fed a diet of GMO corn and soy pellets.

Stock and Broth – Vegetable, Chicken, Beef. Many people assume that stock and broth are interchangeable terms, yet technically speaking, there are some key differences. Stock is typically made with animal bones and some scraps of meat, some aromatics and onions, celery and carrots. It is generally cooked for 2–6 hours and may be slightly gelatinous when cooled. The stock is also left unseasoned.

Conversely, the broth is traditionally made by simmering meat, sometimes with bones but not always, some aromatics, onions, carrots, and celery. It is always seasoned and cooked for under two hours. This yields a thin, flavorful liquid. With the recent rise in popularity of bone broth, this traditional culinary description has changed. We now consider broth to include cooking mainly bones for a long time, sometimes longer than 24 hours, resulting in a rich and nutritious gel-like soup that can be used as a base for sauces, gravies, or enjoyed on its own. Bone broth is an excellent source of minerals and nutrients, helping to heal the digestive tract, promote youthful skin and healthy hair and nails. Vegetable, chicken and beef stock, and broth can easily be made at home with vegetable or meat trimmings, or found at many gourmet grocery stores, often in the freezer section.

Eggs. When selecting eggs, some labels mean more than others, so be sure to purchase the best-quality eggs you can afford. At the top of the list are eggs from pasture-raised hens where the chickens can roam freely, eating what they find in their natural surroundings. While cage-free eggs are a step-up from commercial ones, this designation does not guarantee that the chickens have enjoyed any time outdoors, and were fed a natural, nourishing diet. I recommend purchasing eggs from a local farm at your farmers' market to get a natural, good-quality product that is full of key nutrients such as healthy fats and vitamin D.

Dairy. Cheese, yogurt, and milk are foods that many people commonly purchase commercially, without considering the benefits of organic or grass fed. Also, we've been convinced over the years that low-fat dairy is the healthy option. Neither of these could be further from the truth. Just like meat products, purchasing the best-quality dairy you can afford is of utmost importance. Whole milk from organic, grass-fed cows contains 147% more omega-3s than commercially farmed milk. For the healthiest choice, always opt for full-fat dairy products. Low-fat dairy, as in low-fat yogurt, is often packed with sugar and artificial thickeners to make up for the lack of fatty flavor and texture. We now know that fat is good for us, and eating small amounts of healthy full-fat dairy is a better choice than low-fat dairy options.

Non-Dairy Options. For those who are lactose intolerant or may experience allergy-like symptoms when eating dairy, we are fortunate to have a wide variety of non-dairy alternatives at most grocery stores. These include non-dairy milk such as almond, cashew, coconut, and hemp, as well as coconut yogurt. New products like tigernut and pea milk are hitting the market every day. Always read the ingredient labels to ensure that these products are not packed with preservatives and thickeners like carrageenan and sweeteners.

Fruits and Vegetables

Being a nutritionist, lots of people ask me for the secret to being healthy. If I had to pick just one thing, it would be variety. I am a huge advocate of eating a varied diet. No matter how healthy food is, if we eat the same things over and over again, we will not be able to get the maximum amount of nutrients our bodies need to thrive.

One of Mother Nature's greatest miracles is the many assorted varieties of fruits and vegetables available each season. By selecting seasonal produce, we will not only eat the way nature intended, we will also receive the vital nutrients we need for that given time of the year. Selecting seasonal produce also means you'll save money, support local armers and enjoy the benefits of the tastiest, most nutritious food available. And it will give you that variety in your diet I'm talking about.

Of course, depending on where in the world you live, you may not be able to get fresh, local produce year round. In many parts of North America, it is just too cold to grow anything during the snowy winter months, so it is all the more important to take advantage of seasonal produce when it is available. We can also continue to benefit from seasonal produce by preserving food through jarring, pickling, or freezing. I love to make my fresh tomato sauce at the end of the summer and freeze fresh berries and peaches when they are in season, so I can benefit from summer's bounty during the cold winter months.

Below are a few of my favorite fruits and vegetables, the ones I try always to have on hand. While I may not purchase them every time I go to the store, I try to cycle through these staples, working with what's available seasonally, to maximize my family's intake of nutrients and enjoy the delicious flavors. I also like to mix in one or two new fruits or vegetables each week so that... even our variety is varied!

Fruits	**Vegetables**	
Berries	Spinach	Baby potatoes
Tomatoes	Kale	Sweet potatoes
Oranges	Cabbage	Onions
Lemons	Broccoli	Garlic
Limes	Cauliflower	Ginger
Apples	Carrots	Beets
Grapefruit	Leeks	
Bananas	Asparagus	
Avocados	Romaine	

Let's not forget herbs! Many people fail to realize that herbs are not just for adding fantastic flavor to meals, they are also packed full of nutrients. Think herb tea? I like to cultivate a little herb garden at home so I can quickly and easily snip fresh herbs for my recipes. Some of my favorites include parsley, cilantro, mint, thyme, sage, rosemary, basil, and dill.

THE REAL FOOD KITCHEN EQUIPMENT ESSENTIALS

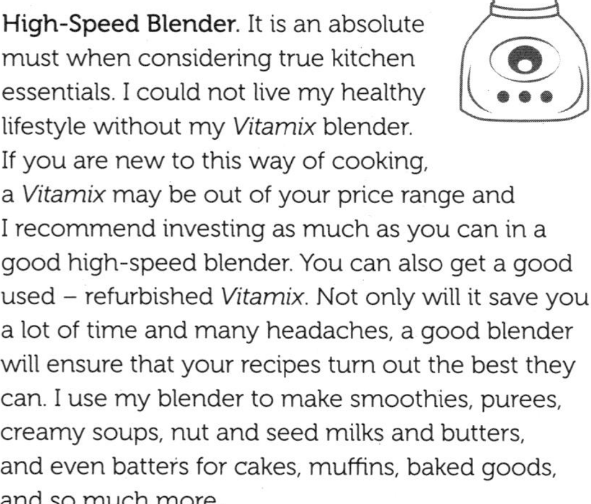

Now, on to the tools I find most useful in the kitchen.

High-Speed Blender. It is an absolute must when considering true kitchen essentials. I could not live my healthy lifestyle without my *Vitamix* blender. If you are new to this way of cooking, a *Vitamix* may be out of your price range and I recommend investing as much as you can in a good high-speed blender. You can also get a good used – refurbished *Vitamix*. Not only will it save you a lot of time and many headaches, a good blender will ensure that your recipes turn out the best they can. I use my blender to make smoothies, purees, creamy soups, nut and seed milks and butters, and even batters for cakes, muffins, baked goods, and so much more.

Food Processor. This is the second and only other kitchen essential I recommend you invest in. A good food processor can save you time and energy when chopping and grating vegetables and fruits, as well as grinding whole nuts and seeds, making energy balls, mashing cooked vegetables and mixing batters. It offers versatility during food prep, and while it does not yield a super smooth texture like a blender, it's an excellent tool for when you need to chop ingredients into a coarse texture.

Pressure Cooker. Our grandmothers swore by this kitchen essential, and pressure cookers have recently enjoyed a mega-revival. Also known as the Instant Pot, food is cooked under pressure at a high temperature which simulates a long braising process. Instant Pots have become the busy family's new best friend as they allow food that would typically take long hours cooking on the stove to be whipped up in minutes. Instant Pot recipes include a variety of vegetable and meat stews, Indian dishes such as butter chicken, lentil curries, quick bone broths, and many more.

Cutting Boards are a kitchen staple, yet many people are confused as to what kind of cutting board they should use. Plastic, wood, and glass are just some of the options out there, but which one is the most sanitary, easiest to clean, and won't damage your knives? While plastic may seem like the more sanitary option, studies show that knife-scarred plastic cutting boards are impossible to clean and can harbor tons of bacteria. Besides, they are bad for the environment, and those knife scars mean that small amounts of plastic are getting into your food.

Wood is a good option and especially easy on knives. If properly cared for, a wooden cutting board can last you for many years. Be sure to handwash your board and protect with food-grade mineral oil. Also, beware of purchased "butcher block" wooden boards that have pieces glued together using toxic glues. Instead, opt for a good maple or beech cutting board that's a single piece. Tempered glass cutting boards are a great sanitary option. They are easy to clean and dishwasher safe, but they will quickly dull even the sharpest of knives.

Parchment Paper/Silicon Mats. A nonstick cover like parchment paper or a silicon baking mat can go a long way toward easing clean up. If using parchment paper, purchase the unbleached brown variety as the white parchment paper is often treated with chemicals. Food-grade silicon mats, like Silpat mats, are another great alternative and a more cost-effective option, because they can be used over and over again.

Slow Cooker. This tool is incredibly handy for busy home chefs. Also known as a Crock Pot, it can also be used to keep dishes warm during large gatherings. While you may not use it all the time, slow cookers are generally inexpensive and a handy tool to have if you have space in your kitchen cupboards. Crock pots are a very affordable option for your real food kitchen.

Sharp Knives. A good set of sharp knives is a must. What many people don't realize is that you can cut yourself more often and more severely with a blunt knife than a sharp one. It's essential to purchase a good set of knives, and if properly cared for, they can last you a lifetime. If you're used to relying on processed foods, maybe you haven't missed having a good knife block to work with. However, the new way of eating I'm proposing requires a little more prep time and a quality set of knives will help you make the most of every minute.

Pots and Pans. When investing in pots and pans, think about the size of your family and the variety of sizes you will need and use. Be sure to purchase Teflon-free pots and pans that are non-toxic. Ceramic, porcelain, or stainless steel cookware are good options.

Lemon Press. While I can't say a lemon press is a necessity, since lemons and other citrus fruits can be juiced in several different ways, I find that a lemon press extracts the maximum amount of juice and cleans up easily.

Garlic Press. Here's another small luxury I like to have. While mincing garlic using a knife is an option, a garlic press helps save me lots of time and effort. I love using garlic in my recipes, and for a minimal investment, my garlic press makes minced garlic almost completely effortless – load the press and squeeze.

Large Dutch Oven. This item, made of cast iron and enamel like a Staub or Le Creuset, may require a hefty upfront investment, but it will last you a lifetime. I use my Dutch oven for soups, stews, roasts, homemade bread, and so much more.

Heavy Duty Baking Sheets are a must-have in any kitchen. Nonstick baking sheets are sprayed with toxins, so I prefer to use a stainless steel sheet covered with parchment paper or a silicon mat to prevent food from sticking. A good-quality, heavy-duty sheet prevents warping from the high h eat of the oven, so don't go the inexpensive route. I also like my sheets to have a 1–2-inch lip to prevent any oils or juices from escaping and dripping onto the bottom of the oven, making a mess and potentially causing a fire.

Mini and Regular Muffin Tins and Ice Cream Scooper. I love making muffins. They are so versatile – a great snack on the go, a quick breakfast, or an afternoon treat. Savory or sweet, my kids love them as much as I do. Muffin tins can also be used to make mini breakfast quiches, taco cups, and so much more. To prevent sticking, I like to use reusable silicon muffin cups. And if you're asking why the ice cream scooper, here's why: To make sure each muffin is baked to perfection, I use an ice cream scooper to measure the same amount of batter into each cup.

Casserole Dish. Having several large, deep pans with high sides is another must. A ceramic or glass dish is a good option for roasted vegetables, casseroles, and lasagnas. I like to have an extra-large dish for family gatherings, as well as several smaller ones which I use when I'm making a few batches to freeze.

Waffle Iron. At my house, we use our waffle iron all the time. We love waffles, and I like to make a big batch and freeze them for the kids to enjoy on busy school mornings. If you have space for a waffle iron in your kitchen, I highly recommend purchasing one as waffles add a wonderful sense of fun to any meal.

Pepper Mill. Freshly grated pepper is one of life's greatest pleasures. It's so fragrant and flavorful, and just a sprinkle can elevate most dishes. I like to keep a pepper mill within reach so I can freshly grate whole peppercorns and enjoy the freshest peppery flavor.

Glass Storage Containers. A variety of glass storage containers can make life a lot easier. Meal prep is an essential part of my week, since meal prep is the way I ensure that my family has healthy meals throughout the week – no matter how busy we are, and despite any last-minute glitches that might otherwise have us ordering takeout. It takes a variety of containers – ones that store well – to make meal prep a breeze. And as you may have seen in the Meal Prepping chapter, I prefer glass.

References

https://www.ncbi.nlm.nih.gov/pubmed/15735074

Chapter Six

BREAKFAST

As your mom always told you, breakfast is the most important meal of the day. However, what you eat is the biggest consideration. Sugary cereals, white bread with jam, coffee, or processed options will not give your body the support and energy it needs to carry on throughout your busy day. How many of you have eaten a less than nourishing breakfast only to find yourself "hangry" by the time you sit down at your desk.

Our first meal of the day is meant to literally "break" the fast from the night before. Most of us have gone at least 12 hours without eating, therefore the quality and nutrient content of breakfast must include protein, fiber, and healthy fats. I stress the importance of protein first thing in the morning as it supports adrenal glands, energy levels, prevents blood sugar fluctuations, and gives your metabolism a much-needed boost.

This chapter is my favorite of the book as I love breakfast. Whether you choose sweet or savory, this chapter provides many nourishing options from overnight oats, eggs, easy blender pancakes, or avocado toast, there are options for weekday and weekend mornings that can be made ahead of time, batch-prepared or enjoyed on a lazy Saturday morning.

Let your taste buds guide you through these delicious options to jump-start your day.

Smoothies – Nutrition in a Cup

Protein smoothies are one of the easiest ways to pack a powerful punch into a busy morning routine. Protein nourishes the adrenal glands (helps reduce blood sugar cravings, hunger pangs, and stress during the day), while boosting your metabolism. The combinations are endless when it comes to smoothie ingredients, as you'll see below. Just be sure to lay in your supplies so you're always ready to start the day right!

Nothing's simpler. Blend it up, put it in your cup, and get yourself off to another great day! Here are a few of my favorite smoothie and smoothie bowl combinations – the options are endless.

Pick Your Liquid

Water

Coconut water

Coconut milk

Almond or other nut milk

Oat milk

Add Protein

Vegan – plant blends
See resource guide for recommended brands

Fermented greens and protein
See resource guide for recommended brands

Whey

Nuts, seeds

Nut butters

Flavor with Fruit (fresh or frozen)

Berries

Pineapple

Mango

Bananas

Go Green for Vitamins

Choose spinach or kale, even lettuce, parsley, or cilantro!

Sprinkle in a Nutrition Boost

Turmeric

Ginger

Cinnamon

Hemp seeds

Ground flaxseeds

Chia seeds

Bee pollen

Cacao powder

Coconut flakes

Omega-3 oils
See resource guide for recommended brands

Coconut oil

MCT oil

Aloe vera

Drizzle in Some Sweetness *(optional)*

Honey

Dates

Maple Syrup

Seasonal Smoothies

Servings: *1*	Prep time: *10 mins*	Cook time: *n/a*

Mango Strawberry Pre-Workout Smoothie

1 cup unsweetened almond milk

1 cup fresh hulled strawberries

1 cup frozen mango

1 Tbsp hemp seeds

2 Tbsp fresh squeezed lemon juice

6 cubes of ice

1 scoop Fermented Organic Greens – chocolate flavor (optional) *See resource guide for recommended brands*

Optional toppings

Hemps seeds, mulberries,
and fresh-sliced strawberries

Directions

1 Starting with the almond milk, combine all the ingredients in a blender and blend until smooth.

2 Add more almond milk if you prefer to thin out the smoothie.

Green Tropical Smoothie

⅓ cup coconut milk

¼ cup Greek yogurt

1 cup frozen pineapple

⅓ cup frozen mango

1 frozen banana

2 cups fresh kale of any kind

1 Tbsp flaxseeds

1 scoop Fermented Organic Greens – Tropical flavor (optional) *See resource guide for recommended brands*

Topping

Shredded coconut

Directions

1 Place all the ingredients in a blender and blend until smooth.

2 I used shredded coconut as the topping to give a crunch, but feel free to add any fun toppings you like.

Citrus & Greens Energizing Smoothie

½ cup full-fat coconut milk

½ cup coconut water

1 frozen banana

½ medium grapefruit

1 large orange

1 tsp chia seeds

1 tsp hemps seeds

1 tsp flaxseeds

Juice of half a medium lemon

2 cups fresh spinach

½ cup ice

1 scoop Fermented Organic Greens – unflavored (optional) *See resource guide for recommended brands*

Toppings

Orange zest and hemp seeds

Directions

1 Starting with the coconut water and coconut milk, add all the ingredients in a high-speed blender. Blend until smooth.

2 Serve in a cup. Add a splash of hemp seeds and orange zest, enjoy!

Healing Turmeric Smoothie

Servings: *1*	**Prep time:** *5 mins*	**Cook time:** *n/a*

Ingredients

1 cup canned coconut milk

½ frozen banana

½ cup fresh pineapple

1 tsp coconut oil

1 tsp turmeric powder

1 tsp fresh ginger

1 Tbsp flaxseeds

Directions

1. Blend all the ingredients in a high-speed blender until smooth.
2. Serve in your favorite cup, sprinkle with more turmeric powder, and enjoy!

Berry-Banana Oat Smoothie

Servings: *1*	Prep time: *5 mins*	Cook time: *n/a*

Ingredients

Banana-oat layer

1 frozen banana (or fresh and then add ice cubes)

¼ cup gluten-free rolled oats

¼ cup coconut yogurt

⅓ cup almond milk

1 tsp honey

Berry layer

½ cup coconut milk (canned)

½ cup frozen mixed berries

1 Tbsp chia seeds

Directions

1. For each layer, add all the ingredients to a blender and blend until smooth.
2. Make sure to wash the blender in between each use so that each mixture stays its own color.
3. When ready to serve, fill up the serving cup with the banana-oat mixture first and then add the berry layer. It just makes it pretty to eat!

GF V DF

Berry Smoothie Bowl

Servings: *1*	**Prep time:** *10 mins*	**Cook time:** *n/a*

Ingredients

1 cup frozen mixed berries

¼ cup full-fat coconut milk

½ cup unsweetened almond milk

1 scoop Fermented Organic Protein & Greens – vanilla flavor (optional)
See resource guide for recommended brands

¼ cup ice

Optional toppings

Hemp seeds
Frozen or fresh berries
Edible flowers

Directions

1. Place all ingredients in a blender and mix until smooth.
2. Add all your fun toppings and enjoy!

Chocolate Peanut Butter Smoothie Bowl

Servings: *1*	**Prep time:** *10 mins*	**Cook time:** *n/a*

Ingredients

¼ almond milk

½ cup coconut yogurt

1½ frozen banana, diced

1 Tbsp natural peanut butter, no sugar added

1 Tbsp cacao powder

1 Tbsp chia seeds

1 scoop Fermented Organic Protein & Greens – chocolate flavor or Vegan Protein – chocolate flavor (optional)
See resource guide for recommended brands

Optional toppings

Sliced banana
Bee pollen
Granola
Peanut butter
Cacao nibs

Directions

1. Add all the ingredients into a high-speed blender, blend until smooth and thick to allow toppings to sit on top.
2. Serve in a bowl and add all your favorite toppings.

Overnight Oats

Overnight oats and chia seed puddings have become so popular, and for good reason. They are super quick to put together, and there is no cooking involved. I usually prepare mine in the evening while I'm cleaning up dinner dishes. I make two or three days' worth and enjoy them at breakfast or for a snack. The combinations are endless and I've included a few topping options in this recipe, but let your taste buds and the season guide your bowl.

Servings: *2*	**Prep time:** *5 mins*	**Cook time:** *5 h or overnight*

Ingredients

1½ cups rolled oats

1½ cup full-fat coconut milk

½ cup filtered water

¼ cup maple syrup

¼ cup shredded coconut

3 Tbsp hempseeds

Optional toppings

- Sliced banana
- Peaches, apricots, pears, apples
- Berries – blueberries, raspberries, strawberries
- Dried goji berries
- Cacao nibs
- Shredded coconut
- Maple syrup
- Any types of seeds or nuts (e.g., chia seeds, pumpkin seeds, Brazil nuts, etc.)

Directions

1. In a large mason jar, mix together the oats, coconut milk, water, maple syrup, shredded coconut, and hemp seeds. Stir to combine.
2. Store in the fridge overnight (with the lid on, preferably an airtight container).
3. When you are ready to serve the next day, stir the mixture one more time to combine. Serve in a bowl with your favorite toppings from the list above. Enjoy!

Chocolate-Almond Butter Chia Pudding

Chia pudding is one of the easiest breakfasts to prepare, and the brilliant part is it can be made the night before and put in the fridge for you to enjoy the next morning. Chia seeds are like black magic – they are a true superfood and filled with healthy fats, protein, and fiber. When left to soak in any liquid they swell and gel, making them a great thickening agent, and a wonderful food for healthy digestion.

Servings: *4*	**Prep time:** *10 mins*	**Cook time:** *1 h + (setting time)*

Ingredients

Chocolate-almond butter layer

- 1 cup almond milk
- 4 Tbsp almond butter
- 3 Tbsp coconut nectar (or use maple syrup)
- 2 Tbsp raw cacao powder – unsweetened
- ¼ cup chia seeds
- ¼ tsp vanilla powder
- Pinch of Himalayan pink salt

Chia seeds layer

- 1 cup coconut milk
- 2–3 Tbsp coconut nectar
- ¼ cup chia seeds
- 2 Tbsp unsweetened shredded coconut

Directions

1. In a bowl, whisk together all of the ingredients in the chocolate almond butter layer. Let gel for about 10 minutes, and then transfer to a blender. Blend until smooth. Remove from blender into a bowl and set aside.
2. For the chia seed layer combine all the ingredients in a bowl and let sit for about 15 minutes to form gel.
3. Once both layers are made, layer the chocolate almond butter and chia seeds puddings in small jars or serving cups, alternating as desired. Refrigerate for at least 1 hour before serving.
4. Top it off with more almond butter, frozen raspberry, or chocolate chips, and serve!

Tip: My favorite blend is chia with coconut milk (always canned coconut milk), and a bit of natural sweetener such as maple syrup, honey, or coconut nectar. I created this recipe to be extra decadent with a delicious layer of almond butter – if you have extra time go ahead and make this, and layer it in a glass dish – pretty food tastes so good. But if you are in a hurry (like we are most mornings), then simply add a spoonful of almond butter and sprinkle on your favorite toppings. The combinations are endless.

Peach-Apricot Chia Jam

As soon as the end of July hits, and the Okanagan is bursting with tree fruits, my breakfasts and desserts become the sweetest treats ever. Not sure if there is anything more delicious than a freshly picked peach. Well, that's before you enjoyed it mixed with apricot and turned into this delicious jam. The chia seeds take the place of pectin and make an incredible fibrous-binding agent rich in omega-3 healthy fats and protein.

Servings: *3*	**Prep time:** *10 mins*	**Cook time:** *15 mins*

Ingredients

6 large peaches, peeled and roughly chopped

6 medium apricot, roughly chopped

¼ cup water

½ juice of a lemon

½ juice of an orange

4 Tbsp chia seeds, white or black

Pinch of sea salt

1 tsp vanilla extract

4 Tbsp raw honey

Directions

1. In a medium saucepan heat the peaches and apricots along with the water, juice of the lemon and orange.
2. Bring it to a boil and lower to simmer for about 10 minutes.
3. Using a potato masher, mash the fruit mixture in the saucepan. Don't make the whole mixture into a puree, leave some pieces of the apricot and peach in there.
4. Stir in the chia seeds, salt, vanilla extracts, and honey. Remove from the heat and allow to cool while the mixture thickens.
5. Transfer the jam into an airtight glass container and store in the fridge.
6. Enjoy the jam within 10 days.

Tip: Use on toast, in your oatmeal, or as a filling for my spelt thumbprint cookies, you will never want to buy store-made jam again.

Protein Banana Blender Pancakes

Pancakes in 5 minutes with no whisking or stirring. Sign me up. And that's exactly what these protein banana blender pancakes deliver. Use a high-speed blender, add all your ingredients and you have batter ready in under 5 minutes. These pancakes are so quick to make that I often prepare them for the kids before school – imagine pancakes from scratch before you leave for work or school.

Servings: *8+*	**Prep time:** *5 mins*	**Cook time:** *6–7 mins (per pancake)*

Ingredients

2 cups rolled oats

1 egg

2 cups almond milk

1 Tbsp chia seeds

1 banana

1 scoop of your favorite protein powder

Coconut oil for cooking

Directions

1. Add all ingredients in a high-speed blender. Blend for 1 minute. Let sit for 5 minutes to allow chia seeds to swell and thicken the batter.
2. Heat 1 tablespoon of coconut oil over medium heat. Wipe away any excess oil (too much oil will cause uneven burning of pancakes).
3. Pour ¼ cup of the batter at a time to form pancakes. Let cook 2–3 minutes per side and flip. Make sure pancakes are fully cooked.
4. These freeze very well. I recommend placing a small sheet of parchment paper between each pancake so they don't stick. Wrap in plastic wrap and store in a large freezer bag. Place in toaster when ready to eat.

Tip: The chia, rolled oats, and protein powder (optional) make these extra satisfying and will knock out any mid-morning cravings.

Apple-Cinnamon Multigrain Pancakes

Just by reading these ingredients you can smell the aroma of a freshly baked, warm apple pie, only in this case they are nourishing apple cinnamon pancakes. My kids absolutely love these pancakes, and they are a real treat for the eye with the apple in the middle.

Servings: *8*	**Prep time:** *20 mins*	**Cook time:** *3 mins per batch*

Ingredients

1 apple

1½ tsp ground cinnamon, divided

1 cup whole wheat flour

½ cup quick cook oats

¼ tsp salt

4 tsp baking powder

1 large egg

1½ cup milk or you can use any plant milk of your choice (coconut or almond)

3 Tbsp coconut sugar

¼ cup plain Greek yogurt

1 tsp vanilla extract

Coconut oil for cooking

Directions

1. Core apple using an apple corer or with a pairing knife. Slice apple into ⅛–¼-inch rounds. Place in a small bowl, sprinkle with ½ teaspoon cinnamon and toss to coat. Set aside.
2. In a large bowl, whisk together flour, oats, salt, baking powder, and remaining 1 teaspoon cinnamon until well combined.
3. In a separate medium bowl, whisk together egg, milk, coconut sugar, yogurt, and vanilla extract.
4. Make a well in the center of dry ingredients and add wet ingredients. Using a rubber spatula, gently fold ingredients together until just combined. A few little lumps of flour are ok. It is important not to overmix the batter or the pancakes will be tough and dense.
5. Heat a griddle or a large nonstick frying pan over medium heat. Drizzle about 1 teaspoon oil in pan, let warm for 1 minute and add 1–2 apple rings.
6. Allow apples to soften, turning once if desired, about 1 minute. Pour ¼ cup of pancake batter over apples and let it spread to fully cover the apple slices. Cook until bubbles begin to form on the surface of the pancake and the edges look dry, about 1 minute.
7. Using a spatula carefully flip pancake and cook about another 2 minutes until cooked through. Repeat with remaining apple rings and pancake batter. Enjoy pancakes while warm.

Ricotta-Pumpkin Pancakes

These pancakes are irresistible, especially when served with a decadent chocolatey maple drizzle. If you are avoiding dairy, you could sub the ricotta for coconut yogurt which is also creamy and delicious.

Servings: *4*	**Prep time:** *15 mins*	**Cook time:** *15 mins*

Ingredients

1¼ cups whole wheat pastry flour

2 tsp baking powder

½ tsp baking soda

½ tsp cinnamon

¼ tsp salt

½ cup ricotta cheese

½ cup pumpkin puree

1 large egg

2 large egg whites

1 tsp orange zest

⅓ cup almond, rice, or hemp milk

1 Tbsp melted coconut oil, plus extra for cooking

Carob-maple syrup

½ cup pure maple syrup

2 Tbsp water

⅓ cup carob powder

Directions

1. Stir together maple syrup and water in a bowl. Sieve carob powder overtop and whisk until well combined. If too thick, adjust consistency of syrup with a little extra water. Set aside while making pancakes.
2. In a large bowl, whisk together flour, baking powder, baking soda, cinnamon, and salt.
3. In another bowl, whisk together ricotta cheese, pumpkin puree, egg, egg whites, orange zest, milk, and melted coconut oil until well combined.
4. With a spatula, gently fold the wet mixture into the dry mixture until just incorporated. It is important not to overmix or pancakes will be flat and tough instead of light and fluffy.
5. Heat a griddle or large nonstick frying pan over medium-low heat. Add a little coconut oil and swirl to coat the bottom of the pan. Working in batches, pour a scant ¼ cup of batter onto griddle. Cook until bubbles start to appear and edges look dry. Flip and continue cooking for another 2 minutes. Transfer to a plate and continue cooking pancakes, using more coconut oil as needed.

Tip: When ready to serve, divide pancakes among serving plates and drizzle with carob maple syrup. Garnish with fresh fruit, such as raspberries, blueberries, or sliced banana, if desired.

Lemon-Blueberry Waffles

Lemon juice and zest give such a fresh delight to baked goods, including waffles and pancakes. I love serving these lemon waffles for a weekend brunch with friends, as they are a real crowd-pleaser. The blueberries are so vibrant with the lemon, but any berry would work. As with any pancake or waffle recipe, I highly recommend doubling your batch so that you have extra to freeze. They can be easily put into the toaster for your busy weekday mornings.

Servings: *7–8*	**Prep time:** *10 mins*	**Cook time:** *5 mins per batch*

Ingredients

Dry ingredients

- 1 cup whole wheat or spelt flour
- 1 cup oat flour
- 1 Tbsp organic cane sugar
- 2 tsp baking powder
- 1 tsp baking soda
- Pinch of salt

Wet ingredients

- 2 eggs
- 1¼ cup coconut milk
- ¼ cup melted coconut oil
- ¼ cup maple syrup
- Juice and rind of 2 medium lemons
- ¼–½ cup fresh or frozen blueberries

Directions

1. In a medium bowl, combine together the dry ingredients as listed above.
2. In a small bowl, mix wet ingredients.
3. Add the wet ingredients to the dry bowl ingredients and mix well.
4. Fold in blueberries.
5. After preheating your waffle maker, scoop out the waffle mixture and add onto the waffle iron. Cook until the edges are crisp and the color is golden brown.
6. Serve with sliced banana and maple syrup. Enjoy!

Carrot-Apple Waffles

These waffles are a take on my *Morning Glory Muffins* (which is my all-time favorite muffin – see page 77), packed full of carrots, apples, and just so happens to be the most delicious way to start your Saturday morning. Serve with all your favorite toppings.

Servings: *8*	**Prep time:** *20 mins*	**Cook time:** *5 mins per batch*

Ingredients

2 cups spelt flour

2 tsp baking soda

2 Tbsp ground flaxseeds

1 Tbsp ground chia seeds

¼ cup chopped walnuts

1 tsp cinnamon

1 cup grated carrots

½ cup grated apples

2 cups coconut milk

¼ cup melted coconut oil

1 tsp vanilla extract

2 Tbsp maple syrup

Pinch of sea salt

Directions

1. In a medium bowl, combine together the spelt flour, baking soda, ground flaxseeds, ground chia seeds, chopped walnuts, and cinnamon.
2. In a small bowl, mix together grated apples and carrots, coconut milk, coconut oil, vanilla extract, maple syrup, and sea salt.
3. Add the wet ingredients to the dry bowl ingredients and mix well.
4. After preheating your waffle maker, scoop out the waffle mixture and add onto the waffle iron. Cook until the edges are crisp and the color is golden brown.
5. Serve with berries and extra maple syrup. Enjoy!

Morning Glory Muffins

Get ready to say a happy and cheery good morning with these classic morning glory muffins. This is a recipe I brought to the West Coast, and have continually adapted and tweaked to come up with the most delicious and nutritious version of this flavorful and moist muffin. These are delicious for breakfast, snack, or make a beautiful addition to your brunch.

Servings: *12 (or 24 mini)*	**Prep time:** *20 mins*	**Cook time:** *20 mins*

Ingredients

Dry ingredients

- 2 cups sprouted spelt flour
- ½ cup coconut sugar
- ½ cup shredded coconut
- 2 tsp baking soda
- 1 teaspoon baking powder
- ¼ tsp salt
- 2 tsp cinnamon

Wet ingredients

- ½ cup maple syrup
- ½ cup melted coconut oil, room temperature
- 2 tsp vanilla
- 2 eggs, well beaten
- 2 cups grated carrots
- 1 medium shredded zucchini
- 1 apple, peeled and grated
- ¼ cup raisins
- ¼ cup dark chocolate chips

Directions

1. Preheat oven to 350 °F (175 °C).
2. Mix flour, baking soda, baking powder, salt, and cinnamon together in a bowl. Set aside.
3. Beat eggs. Add maple syrup, oil, and vanilla to beaten eggs. Beat together until light and fluffy.
4. Add wet ingredients to dry ingredients. Fold in the carrots, zucchini, apples, raisins, and chocolate chips. Don't overmix.
5. Place in greased or lined muffin tins. Bake at 350 °F for 20 mins or until toothpick inserted comes out clean.
6. Let cool in pan for about 10 minutes, then transfer to a wire rack to finish cooling.

Banana-Walnut Muffin

A classic and timeless muffin that can be enjoyed any season for breakfast or a nourishing snack. The oat flour provides a smooth, earthy mouthfeel, while the banana and walnut go together perfectly creating a simple and nutritious bite of flavor.

Servings: *12 muffins*	**Prep time:** *10 mins*	**Cook time:** *20 mins*

Ingredients

Dry ingredients

- 2 cups oat flour
- 1 cup rolled oats
- 1 tsp baking powder
- ½ tsp baking soda
- Pinch of sea salt
- ½ cup chopped walnuts

Wet ingredients

- 2 eggs
- 3 medium bananas, mashed
- ¼ cup maple syrup
- ¼ cup coconut oil, melted
- 1 tsp vanilla extract

Toppings

- 2 Tbsp rolled oats
- 1 Tbsp coconut sugar

Directions

1. Preheat oven to 325 ˚F (165 ˚C). Coat a muffin tray with nonstick spray and set aside.
2. In a large bowl combine oat flour, rolled oats, baking soda, baking powder, and salt.
3. In a medium bowl whisk the eggs. Add in the maple syrup, mashed bananas, coconut oil, and vanilla extract.
4. Add the wet ingredients to the dry ingredients bowl and combine. Fold in the walnuts.
5. Pour the batter evenly into the prepared muffin pan. Sprinkle with rolled oats and coconut sugar.
6. Bake for 17–20 minutes or until a toothpick comes out clean.
7. Allow to cool completely and serve.

Tip: Store in an airtight container for up to 4 days.

Breakfast Power Cookies

Cookies for breakfast – yes please! Let your inner kid smile brightly in the morning with these nourishing and complete breakfast power cookies. Loaded with protein, healthy fats, and lots of fiber, these cookies make the perfect replacement for cereal, or toast, and can be eaten while on the go. They freeze really well, so double the batch and keep on hand for those extra-busy weeks.

Servings: *21*	**Prep time:** *15 mins*	**Cook time:** *20 mins*

Ingredients

Dry ingredients

- 1½ cup oat flour
- ¾ cup rolled oats
- ½ cup almond meal flour (ground from almonds)
- ½ cup chopped walnuts
- ½ cup shredded coconut
- ¼ cup chocolate chips
- ¼ cup raisins
- ½ tsp baking soda
- ½ tsp baking powder
- Pinch of salt

Wet ingredients

- 1 ripe banana
- ¼ almond butter
- ¼ cup coconut oil
- ¼ cup maple syrup
- 1 tsp vanilla extract
- 2 Tbsp flaxseeds + 6 Tbsp water

Directions

1. Preheat oven to 350 °F (175 °C).
2. In a small bowl, combine flaxseeds and water; let rest for 5 minutes. You want this mixture to become thick.
3. Mash in the bananas in the flaxseeds bowl until well combined, and then add in all the remaining wet ingredients.
4. In a medium bowl, combine all the dry ingredients together until well combined.
5. Mix together the wet and dry mixture. Refrigerate for 5 minutes to harden.
6. Drop a spoonful of the cookie mixture on a greased baking sheet. Note they won't expand much in size.
7. Bake for 17–20 minutes or until the cookies are slightly golden brown.
8. Let rest on baking sheet for a few minutes before transferring to a cooling rack. After completely cooled, store in an airtight container to keep fresh for up to a few days.
9. Can keep frozen for up to a month.

Tropical Granola

This granola is wonderful for breakfast, as a snack or dessert. Customize your own granola by using other dried fruits such as blueberries, cranberries, and figs. Granola is delicious served with rice, almond, or hemp milk. Also try it sprinkled over Greek yogurt or frozen yogurt for a more decadent treat.

Servings: *8*	**Prep time:** *15 mins*	**Cook time:** *30 mins*

Ingredients

2 cups old-fashioned rolled oats

1 cup quick-cooking oats

1 cup brown rice crisp cereal

¼ cup ground flaxseeds

¾ cup pureed or well-mashed ripe bananas (about 2 bananas)

2 Tbsp coconut oil, melted

¼ cup pure maple syrup

1 tsp vanilla extract

½ tsp sea salt

1 tsp ground cinnamon

¼ tsp ground nutmeg

¾ cup natural sliced almonds

¾ cup raw pumpkin seeds

½ cup raw, shelled, unsalted sunflower seeds

½ cup hemp hearts

⅓ cup chopped, unsweetened, unsulfured dried mango

⅓ cup chopped, unsulfured dried apricots

½ cup unsweetened coconut flakes, toasted

Directions

1. Preheat oven to 300 °F (150 °C). Line a rimmed baking sheet with parchment paper and set aside.
2. In a large bowl, stir together oats, cereal, and flaxseeds.
3. In another bowl, whisk together banana, coconut oil, maple syrup, vanilla extract, salt, cinnamon, and nutmeg.
4. Pour the wet ingredients over the oat mixture and stir until well combined. Spread mixture onto prepared baking sheet and bake for 30 minutes, stirring granola every 10 minutes.
5. Stir in almonds, pumpkin seeds, sunflower seeds, and hemp hearts. Continue to bake, stirring every 10 minutes, until granola is golden brown, about another 20–30 minutes. Let granola cool completely on baking sheet before stirring in mango, apricots, and coconut.
6. Stored in an airtight container, granola will keep for 2 weeks, if it lasts that long!

Fall Spiced Granola

Once you make granola yourself, you will never buy it again. The fragrant smell of oats and nuts roasting will fill your home with the most mouth-watering aroma. I recommend doubling the batch as it stores well and will become a quick and easy go-to for morning parfaits with your favorite yogurt, or enjoyed as a cereal with milk.

Servings: *8–10*	**Prep time:** *15 mins*	**Cook time:** *25 mins*

Ingredients

3 cups of gluten-free rolled oats

2 cups of pecans

¾ cup pumpkin puree

3 Tbsp melted coconut oil

½ cup maple syrup

1 tsp cinnamon

¼ tsp cloves

½ tsp nutmeg

½ tsp ginger powder

Directions

1. Preheat oven to 325 °F (165 °C).
2. In a large bowl, mix the rolled oats with pecans, cinnamon, cloves, nutmeg, and ginger powder.
3. In a small bowl, mix together melted coconut oil, pumpkin puree, and maple syrup. Pour this over the oat mixture and mix well until everything is coated.
4. Spread the mixture evenly onto a baking sheet and bake for 25 minutes. Give it a stir halfway during the cooking time.
5. Remove from the oven once its golden brown and let cool completely.
6. Store in an airtight container for up to 2 weeks.
7. Enjoy with your favorite milk or yogurt!

Vanilla Pear & Almond-Baked Oatmeal

I love baked oatmeal (even more than regular cooked oatmeal); it reminds me of a breakfast crisp. It's delicious served while warm, topped with an additional splash of almond milk and some chopped fruit or toasted almonds. Make extra and serve as a quick weekday breakfast.

Servings: *4*	**Prep time:** *15 mins*	**Cook time:** *35 mins*

Ingredients

2 cups almond milk

½ cup almond butter

3 Tbsp maple syrup

2 tsp vanilla extract

¼ tsp salt

1 tsp ground cinnamon

¼ tsp ground nutmeg

2 ripe pears, diced

2 cups old-fashioned oats

Directions

1 Preheat oven to 375 °F (190 °C).

2 In a large bowl, whisk together almond milk, almond butter, maple syrup, vanilla extract, salt, cinnamon, and nutmeg until smooth.

3 Add diced pear and oats, and stir to combine.

4 Transfer to a 1½-quart baking dish and bake until set and edges are beginning to brown, about 35 minutes.

5 Serve while warm topped with an additional splash of almond milk, and some chopped fruit or toasted almonds.

Baked Eggs in Spicy Tomato Sauce

If you've never made baked eggs before, you might never make them another way again. A shakshuka makes a delicious weekend breakfast, or brunch item and in my opinion eggs for dinner are always a good idea! Served alongside a warmed loaf of sourdough or pita bread, the tomato sauce is so delicious for dipping.

Servings: *4*	**Prep time:** *10 mins*	**Cook time:** *40 mins*

Ingredients

1 Tbsp grapeseed oil or avocado oil

1 large yellow onion, chopped

1 bell pepper, any color, seeded and chopped

2 garlic cloves, minced

1 tsp ground cumin

1 tsp paprika

¼ tsp dried oregano

¼ tsp red pepper flakes (optional)

½ tsp salt

½ tsp ground black pepper

8 vine ripened tomatoes, chopped

½ cup canned crushed tomatoes

½ cup frozen green peas

½ cup frozen greens, such as chopped kale, Swiss chard, or spinach

4–6 large eggs

2 Tbsp crumbled feta cheese

2 Tbsp chopped fresh dill fronds or parsley leaves

Directions

1. Preheat oven to 325 °F (165 °C).
2. Heat oil in a large ovenproof skillet or frying pan over medium heat. Add onions, peppers, garlic, cumin, paprika, oregano, red pepper flakes (if using), salt, and pepper. Cook, stirring often, until onions have softened, about 10 minutes. Stir in chopped tomatoes, crushed tomatoes, peas, and frozen greens. Bring mixture to a simmer and cook, stirring often, until tomato mixture has thickened slightly, about 10 minutes.
3. Using a wooden spoon, create 6 small wells in mixture and crack an egg into each well.
4. Transfer skillet to oven and cook until eggs are just set, about 15–20 minutes. Garnish with feta cheese and chopped dill.
5. Serve with warm pita bread if desired.

Avocado Toast

Gimme avocado everything! I eat an avocado every day. The healthy fats make this creamy fruit absolutely gorgeous for the skin, hair, nails, as well as energy levels, and more. Avocado is great when added to smoothies, made into puddings, sauces, guacamole, or mashed and layered onto your favorite bread or crackers. This is one of the easiest and simplest savory choices for anytime of the day.

Servings: *1*	**Prep time:** *5 mins*	**Cook time:** *n/a*

Ingredients

2 slices sprouted grain toast
(you may use GF toast if you'd prefer)

1 medium ripe avocado, pitted
and skin removed

Juice of a small lime

1 Tbsp avocado oil

¼ tsp salt

Red pepper flakes for topping

Additional toppings

- Hemp seeds
- Sunflower seeds
- Pumpkin seeds
- Microgreens
- Fresh herbs
- Sliced tomatoes
- Cucumber
- Pickles
- Sauerkraut
- Onion
- Poached or fried eggs

Directions

1. Toast the slices of bread until they are just golden brown.
2. In a small bowl, mix together the avocado, lime juice, avocado oil, and salt. Using the back of a fork mash all the ingredients.
3. Add a generous dollop of the smashed avocado on top of each toast and spread.
4. Sprinkle some chili flakes. At this point you may add any other toppings from the list above. Get creative; your taste bud would love it!

SNACKS

I was once a perpetual grazer, choosing to rarely sit down to a full meal, but instead snacking all day. Apples, cheese, yogurt and granola, muffins, roasted chickpeas, you name it. If it was bite-sized and portable, I was in love.

While I still love to snack in order to maintain my energy levels during the day, I favor more structured and complete meals now, with small snacks in between. However, I do ensure I have plenty of healthy snacks on hand. Cut up fruit and vegetables, dips such as hummus and creamy butter bean, energy balls, and nourishing cookies. A little bit of preparation on the weekend ensures the kids' lunches and between-sports snacking is as nutritious as it can be.

This chapter gives you plenty of healthy snack options that are so versatile they can be part of a healthy breakfast, lunch, or served as a treat or dessert.

So let's get snacking!

Fermented Cashew Dip

Creamy, tangy, salty, sweet yet savory, this is the mother of all dips. And the best part is, fermented foods are so incredibly important for the health of your microbiome and digestive system. The more fermented foods we can eat, the better. Other options include good-quality yogurt especially sheep or goat yogurt, miso, tempeh, kombucha, kefir, sauerkraut, etc. Fermented foods act like magic fertilizer for your gut, helping good bacteria to flourish.

Servings: *8+*	**Prep time:** *10 mins*	**Cook time:** *48 h+*

Ingredients

2 cups raw unsalted cashews, soaked in water for 2 h

¾ cup filtered water

½ tsp salt

1 tsp onion powder

3 Tbsp apple cider vinegar

3 cloves garlic

1 Tbsp nutritional yeast

1 plant-based probiotic capsule (minimum 1 billion cfu)

Directions

1. Rinse the soaked cashews and add them to a blender. Add the filtered water, salt, onion powder, apple cider vinegar, garlic, nutritional yeast, and blend until it becomes smooth.
2. Transfer the mixture into a clean glass jar.
3. Open the probiotic capsule and add to the mixture. Using a wooden spoon mix all the powder until there are no clumps left.
4. Cover the jar with cheesecloth and a rubber band to keep in together.
5. Allow to sit out at room temperature away from the direct light for 48 hours (to allow fermentation to happen).
6. Store in the refrigerator for up to a week.

Tip: I love this dip with a seed-type cracker, but can be used as a dip for vegetables, or spread on your favorite bread. And to be honest, it's so addicting you can just eat it straight from the jar with a spoon.

Zio's Fresh Salsa

This salsa is the best to make when tomatoes are at their peak. It takes a bit of chopping, but is so worth the effort as this is truly the best salsa recipe I've ever tried (thank you very much to my brother-in-law, aka Zio). It has been passed down over the years in our family and I'm so happy to share this with you. It pairs great with the guacamole for a fun and casual appetizer or snack.

Servings: *10+*	**Prep time:** *25 mins*	**Cook time:** *n/a*

Ingredients

8 ripe red tomatoes, diced (remove seeds)

2 fresh jalapeños, diced

1 small yellow onion, diced

1 (5 oz) can of tomato paste

5 garlic cloves, minced

1 bunch of cilantro, diced (remove stems)

10 radishes, finely chopped

½ tsp sea salt

Directions

1. You can either chop/dice all ingredients by hand or mix in a food processor. It depends on if you prefer a chunky or saucy salsa.
2. Adjust seasoning with salt to desired taste.

Tip: This recipe freezes well, so double or triple your batch, and enjoy all the fruits of your labor all winter.

Creamy Butter Bean Dip

As the name implies, butter beans have a delicate, buttery texture and are filled with fiber and protein making these an excellent addition to your diet. They can be eaten in so many ways (I've actually made flourless cookies using butter beans), but one of my favorites is as a base for dip. This dip makes an excellent appetizer, or a quick lunch or snack. Dip your favorite tortilla or cracker, and you will feel so satisfied.

Servings: *4*	**Prep time:** *20 mins*	**Cook time:** *n/a*

Ingredients

1 large can (14 oz) butter beans, rinsed and drained

4 garlic cloves, roasted

¼ cup freshly squeezed lemon juice, approximately 2 medium lemons

¼ cup olive oil

¼ cup maple syrup

1 tsp smoked paprika

½ tsp salt

½ tsp black pepper

¼ cup water

Directions

1. Using a high-speed blender or a food processor to mix the butter beans, garlic, lemon juice, olive oil, maple syrup, smoked paprika, salt, and black pepper until smooth.
2. Start by adding one tablespoon of water at a time. If you would like a thicker texture add less water. Adjust the seasoning (I added a little bit more salt at this point).
3. Transfer the butter bean mixture to a serving bowl. Sprinkle with extra paprika and drizzle over extra olive oil. Top with the parsley and thinly sliced lemons. Serve with the flat bread or any kind of crackers you enjoy!

The Best Guacamole

I eat an avocado every day. I usually add avocado to my morning smoothie, and I will often eat on toast or as a snack during the day. Avocado is one of the most beautiful and glorious foods that will make your skin shine from the inside. I didn't realize how much I loved guacamole until my brother-in-law, Adriano, brought it over as an appy one family gathering. OMG, this is serious guacamole love. So on behalf of us, I gift you the BEST guacamole ever.

Servings: *6*	**Prep time:** *15 mins*	**Cook time:** *n/a*

Ingredients

6 avocadoes

1 tomato, chopped finely

½ cup fresh cilantro, diced

1 small yellow onion, finely diced

1–2 limes, juiced

¼ tsp salt

½ small jalapeño, finely diced (optional), if you don't like spice, don't add this

Directions

1. Scoop out avocado and place in bowl. Mash with a fork to keep texture slightly lumpy. Or if you prefer a smooth guac, then mash completely with the back of a spoon.
2. Add other ingredients and mix together.
3. Adjust guac to desired taste with more lime juice and sea salt.

Tip: This guacamole is a must when making my fish tacos.

Roasted Chickpeas

Simple, crunchy, and oh so satisfying, roasted chickpeas is one of the best snacks. The trick to getting them extra crispy/crunchy is to make sure they are very dry before you coat them. But you need to be gentle as you don't want them to crack during the drying process. There are also so many combinations of sweet and savory you could use – garlic, turmeric, or cinnamon and maple syrup. Happy snacking!

Servings: *2*	**Prep time:** *10 mins*	**Cook time:** *40 mins*

Ingredients

1 large can of chickpeas (14 oz), drained and rinsed

2 Tbsp olive oil

Pinch of sea salt and black pepper

Directions

1. Preheat the oven to 450 °F (230 °C). Line a baking sheet with parchment paper and set aside.
2. Gently dry the rinsed chickpeas between clean paper towels to remove any moisture.
3. In a medium bowl, toss the chickpeas with olive oil, salt, and pepper.
4. Spread the chickpeas on the baking sheet, and bake for 30–40 minutes, until golden brown. Watch carefully after the last few minutes to avoid burning.
5. Let cool for a couple minutes before serving.

Roasted Golden Beet Hummus

Servings: *6–8*	**Prep time:** *15 mins*	**Cook time:** *1 h (includes roasting)*

Ingredients

4 medium golden beets, washed and quartered

1 large can (14 oz), chickpeas, drained and rinsed

3 Tbsp tahini

3 garlic cloves

Juice of 2 medium lemons

¼ cup olive oil

½ tsp salt

Pinch of cayenne pepper

3–4 Tbsp water, to thin out the hummus

Directions

1. Preheat oven to 380 °F (195 °C).
2. Place beets on a baking sheet and drizzle with 1 tablespoon olive oil. Bake for 40–45 minutes, until beets are tender. Let cool completely.
3. In a food processor, combine chickpeas, tahini, garlic, lemon juice, the remaining olive oil, salt, cayenne, and beets. Puree until smooth. Add in 1 tablespoon of the water at a time until the desired consistency for hummus is reached.
4. Serve with your favorite veggies, on a slice of toast, with cracker, or a dollop on your salad. Options are unlimited! Enjoy!

Roasted Red Pepper Hummus

There are so many delicious twists on a classic hummus recipe such as my *Roasted Golden Beet Hummus* recipe on page 103 or this creamy and sweet roasted red pepper version. Red peppers are sweet yet savory, and I love the color, consistency, and flavor it brings to hummus.

Servings: *10*	**Prep time:** *10 mins*	**Cook time:** *n/a*

Ingredients

2 medium red peppers, sliced and roasted

1 large can chickpeas (14 oz), drained and rinsed

½ cup tahini

2 garlic cloves

Juice of 3 medium lemons

½ cup olive oil

1 tsp sea salt

¼ tsp black pepper

1 tsp smoked paprika (optional for more taste)

¼ cup warm water + more if needed

Directions

1. Add the roasted red peppers, chickpeas, tahini, lemon juice, olive oil, sea salt, black pepper, smoked paprika, and warm water into a food processor.
2. Pulse the ingredients for about 60 seconds, and then process until smooth. If the mixture seems too thick, add 1 tablespoon of warm water at a time and blend until desired consistency is reached. Taste the mixture and adjust the seasoning if needed.
3. Pour into a serving bowl and chill thoroughly before serving. Hummus will firm up slightly as it chills. Serve with grilled pita bread, pita chips, crackers, or sliced veggies.

Snickers Energy Balls

The combination of bitter, sweet, and salty all rolled into a delicious chocolate, peanut butter ball that tastes like a Snickers bar. The walnuts provide omega-3s which are nourishing for the heart and brain

Servings: *22*	**Prep time:** *15 mins*	**Cook time:** *2 h to refrigerate*

Ingredients

2 cups pitted Medjool dates

1 cup walnuts

½ cup sunflower seeds

¾ cup organic peanut butter

½ cup vanilla protein powder (optional)
See resource guide for recommended brands

3 Tbsp coconut nectar

2 tsp vanilla extract

Pinch of sea salt

2 Tbsp cacao powder, to roll in the balls

Directions

1. In a food processor, combine all ingredients until dough forms. The dough should be very sticky and be held together when pinched between two fingers.
2. Using your hand, roll the dough into 1 tablespoon balls and repeat until the entire mixture is rolled into balls. Then roll each ball into cacao powder until it's slightly covered.
3. Place on a lined baking sheet or plate and chill in the refrigerator for up to 2 hours or overnight.
4. Store in an airtight container for up to 2 weeks or freeze for up to a month.

Omega-3 Energy Balls

Call them bites or balls, either way these nutritious rounds are popular for good reason. Satisfying, nourishing, quick, and easy, they make a great breakfast on the go, or snack.

Servings: *12*	**Prep time:** *10 mins*	**Cook time:** *1 h*

Ingredients

1 cup rolled oats

¾ cup unsweetened shredded coconut

2 Tbsp chia seeds

2 Tbsp hemp seeds

2 Tbsp cacao nibs

1 Tbsp ground flaxseeds

¾ cup almond butter

½ cup honey

Extra shredded coconut to cover the balls

Directions

1. In a large bowl, mix together all the ingredients. Using a spatula, stir and fold until well incorporated.
2. Scoop mixture into your hands and roll into balls (about one tablespoon).
3. Roll each ball into shredded coconut.
4. Refrigerate for 1 hour before serving.

Dried Fruit & Nut Bites

There are so many superfood options of nuts and seeds that can be included when making energy bites. These unbaked, easy and very nutritious snacks are so great to have on hand. They are quick to make and allow you to be creative when rolling up your family's favorite. These are a sure way to make every bite count.

Servings: *14*	**Prep time:** *15 mins*	**Cook time:** *Refrigerate for 1 h*

Ingredients

12 Medjool dates, pitted

1 cup walnuts

½ cup pecans

¼ cup pumpkin seeds

½ cup shredded coconut

½ cup goji berries

1 Tbsp coconut oil

3 Tbsp Fermented Organic Greens, unflavored (optional or any greens/protein powder would work) *See resource guide for recommended brands*

1 tsp vanilla extract

1 tsp matcha powder (optional)

Pinch of sea salt

¼ cup finely chopped unsalted pistachios, for the topping

Directions

1. Place all the ingredients (except pistachios) into a food processor. Process for 2–3 minutes or until finely chopped and blended.
2. Using a cookie scoop, scoop out the mixture. Roll between your hands to create evenly sized balls.
3. When all balls have been rolled, roll them again through the chopped pistachios and press firmly into the balls.
4. Refrigerate for at least an hour before serving.

Healthy Spelt Banana Bread

How many banana bread recipes have you tried? Promise you that this will be the last. Everyone needs a good banana bread recipe, as it's a classic and usually loved by all. I used my favorite flour, oil, and sweetener (maple syrup) in this recipe, and made it vegan by using a flax egg rather than a regular egg. I always double this batch as it freezes really well. Having a delicious banana bread ready at the last minute is always such a treat.

Servings: *8*	**Prep time:** *15 mins*	**Cook time:** *1 h + cooling*

Ingredients

3 large ripe bananas

⅓ cup melted coconut oil

⅔ cup of maple syrup

2 Tbsp ground flaxseed mixed with 6 Tbsp water, let sit for about 10 mins until it thickens (or you can use 2 eggs)

¼ cup almond milk

1 tsp vanilla extract

½ tsp salt

1 tsp baking soda

1 tsp ground cinnamon

1 ¾ cup spelt flour

½ cup of mini chocolate chips

Directions

1. Preheat oven to 325 °F (165 °C). And grease your loaf pain with coconut oil.
2. In a large bowl, whisk maple syrup and melted coconut oil. Add flax egg. Mix well. Then whip in mashed banana and almond milk.
3. Add baking soda, vanilla, salt, and cinnamon, whisk until blended.
4. Use a large wooden spoon and stir in flour until just combined (don't overmix).
5. Add in chocolate chips.
6. Pour batter into loaf pan and sprinkle extra cinnamon on top. Take a knife and draw a zigzag pattern through loaf as it gives a nice swirl effect.
7. Bake at 325 °F for 50–55 minutes or until toothpick comes out clean. Let loaf pan cool for about 15 minutes and then transfer to a wire rack to cool.

Blueberry-Lemon Loaf with Yogurt Drizzle

Light, fresh, and moist, this blueberry lemon loaf is a take on my *Lemon-Blueberry Waffles* on page 73. I love experimenting with different flours and the combination of buckwheat and almond delivers a bit of a nutty taste, but with a moist consistency. The yogurt drizzle is optional, yet I find myself eating it from the bowl with a spoon, it's so yummy. You could also use coconut yogurt rather than Greek yogurt if you prefer.

Servings: *10*	**Prep time:** *20 mins*	**Cook time:** *70 mins*

Ingredients

¾ cup buckwheat flour

1½ cups almond meal

3 tsp baking powder

2 Tbsp black chia seeds, plus extra for garnish

½ tsp salt

3 large eggs

2½ cups plain Greek yogurt, divided

½ cup extra virgin olive oil

½ cup coconut sugar

3 Tbsp finely grated lemon zest, divided

1½ tsp vanilla extract

1½ cups fresh or frozen blueberries

Directions

1. Preheat oven to 325 °F (165 °C). Lightly grease a 9 x 5-inch loaf pan with olive oil and line with parchment paper. Set aside.
2. In a medium bowl, whisk together buckwheat flour, almond meal, baking powder, chia seeds, and salt until well combined. Set aside.
3. In a large bowl, whisk together eggs, 1½ cups yogurt, olive oil, coconut sugar, 2 tablespoons lemon zest and vanilla extract until well combined.
4. Add dry ingredients and stir together with a wooden spoon or spatula until well combined.
5. Fold blueberries into batter before pouring into prepared loaf tin. Bake until a wooden skewer inserted in the center of the loaf comes out clean, about 60–75 minutes.
6. Allow to cool for 20 minutes in the tin before turning the loaf out onto a wire rack to cool completely to room temperature.
7. Meanwhile in a small bowl, stir together remaining 1 cup yogurt and 1 tablespoon lemon zest.
8. When ready to serve, spread yogurt mixture over top of loaf and garnish with a sprinkle of chia seeds, if desired. Cut into slices and enjoy.

Tip: Without the yogurt topping, blueberry lemon loaf may be refrigerated in an airtight container for up to 5 days or frozen for up to 1 month.

Chocolate Zucchini Loaf

Did you know zucchini is botanically considered a fruit? Yet, because of its neutral, earthy flavor, most of us eat it as a veggie. This loaf will become a go-to recipe as never has it been easier to get your family to eat zucchini – and lots of it. Zucchini makes recipes so moist and delicious, and is a nutrient-dense food containing lots of fiber. Chocolate and zucchini are like a unicorn couple, and this recipe is pure magic.

Servings: *8–10*	**Prep time:** *20 mins*	**Cook time:** *55 mins*

Ingredients

2 Tbsp grounded flaxseeds + 6 Tbsp of water

1½ cup whole wheat flour

1 scoop Chocolate Vegan Protein (optional)
See resource guide for recommended brands

1 cup coconut sugar

1 tsp cinnamon

¼ tsp cardamom

1 tsp baking soda

½ tsp baking powder

Pinch of salt

1 cup applesauce

¼ cup melted coconut oil

1 tsp vanilla extract

1 cup shredded zucchini

½ cup chocolate chips

½ cup chopped walnuts

Directions

1. Preheat oven to 350° F (175 °C). Grease an 8 x 4-inch pan and set aside.
2. In a small bowl, combine the flaxseeds and water; set aside for 10 minutes.
3. In a large bowl, mix the whole wheat flour, coconut sugar, cinnamon, cardamom, baking soda, baking powder, and salt.
4. In a medium bowl, mix together the applesauce, coconut oil, vanilla extract, and the flaxseeds mixture.
5. Add the applesauce mixture to the flour mixture until combined.
6. Fold in the shredded zucchini, chocolate chips, and chopped walnuts.
7. Transfer the mixture to the greased pan. Bake for 50–55 minutes. Check at 50 minutes, depending on the type of oven this baking time may vary on average by 5 minutes.
8. Let the loaf cool down before transferring it to a cooling rack.
9. Enjoy with coffee, tea, or on its own.

Strawberry Lemonade

When strawberry season hits, this lemonade makes the most refreshing and healthy drink. It will steal the show at gatherings, birthday parties, and your neighborhood lemonade stand.

Servings: *4*	**Prep time:** *5 mins*	**Cook time:** *n/a*

Ingredients

1½ cup strawberries, top removed

1 cup fresh lemon juice

4 cups cold water

4 Tbsp honey

Directions

1. Using a blender, blend the strawberries with 1 cup of lemon juice until smooth.
2. Add in the water, honey, and blend for 30 seconds.
3. Adjust the sweetness to your taste.
4. Serve cold over ice.

Cucumber Basil Lemonade

Feel cool as a cucumber with this relaxing, refreshing and hydrating cucumber basil lemonade. It combines summer's beauty into a delicious drink.

Servings: *4*	**Prep time:** *5 mins*	**Cook time:** *n/a*

Ingredients

2 cups cucumber, sliced

1 cup fresh lemon juice

2 sprig of basil

4 cups cold water

4 Tbsp honey or maple syrup

Directions

1. Add the sliced cucumber to a blender with the basil, lemon juice, cold water, and honey/maple syrup. Blend until smooth.
2. Adjust the sweetness and serve over ice.
3. Enjoy!

LIBECO

SOUP

Move over chicken noodle soup (ok this is still a family favorite), and say hello to superfoods in a bowl. Creating delicious, nourishing, and warm soups from scratch has been one of the most fun food adventures yet. I honestly didn't realize how easy it was to take cauliflower or peas and turn it into a bowl of hearty goodness. Vegetables and legumes form the bases of the majority of the soups in this chapter. However, that doesn't mean you can't add mini meatballs, or leftover chicken or turkey.

Having good-quality stock (broth) on hand will help you create the best soups possible. I love my *Vegetable Stock* recipe on page 195, which is something I make in large batches and freeze.

I could literally live on creamy soups topped with avocado, hemp seeds, and a drizzle of full-fat coconut milk. My favorite soup to make on Saturday is the *Roasted Heirloom Tomato-Basil Soup* (see page 121). I have a little extra time that morning to slow roast the tomatoes and garlic, creating the coziest and inviting aroma. Who doesn't want to sit down to a bowl of tomato soup, with a grilled cheese sandwich?

These soup recipes make great weekday dinners, Saturday lunch, or even Sunday dinner if you want to spend a little more time relaxing. No matter what meal you choose to make them for, I recommend doubling the batch and then freeze so you have something nourishing on hand to use at a later date.

May the soup be with you!

Roasted Heirloom Tomato-Basil Soup

A good tomato soup is an essential recipe to have on hand especially during the early fall months when tomatoes are at their peak. I absolutely love heirloom tomatoes, those gnarly shaped, oddly colored, large beauties have the most incredible and fresh, sweet flavor, just as a tomato should. Heirloom tomatoes also make for the most delicious salad paired with fresh Burrata or mozzarella cheese, loads of basil, and a drizzle of extra virgin olive oil.

Servings: *4*	**Prep time:** *15 mins*	**Cook time:** *40 mins*

Ingredients

6 medium-sized heirloom tomatoes, cut in halves

1 large onion, diced

2 cloves garlic

¼ cup olive oil + 2 Tbsp

Freshly ground pepper and salt, to season

2 medium carrots, sliced

1 cup vegetable broth

2 cups full-fat coconut milk

½ cup fresh basil leaves

Directions

1. Preheat oven to 400 °F (205 °C).
2. Spread the tomatoes and garlic onto a baking tray.
3. Drizzle with the ¼ cup olive oil and season with salt and pepper. Roast for 20–30 minutes or until everything is caramelized and all the juices are flowing.
4. While the tomatoes are roasting in a large pot, sauté the onion with 2 tablespoons of olive oil, just until they are soft and fragrant.
5. Add the sliced carrots and cook for an additional 5 minutes.
6. Remove the roasted tomatoes and garlic from the oven and transfer to the same pot as the sauté onion and carrots.
7. Add 1 cup of the vegetable stock.
8. Bring to boil and reduce heat to a simmer for 5 minutes.
9. Remove from the heat and add the basil leaves.
10. Using an immersion blender (or transfer to a high-speed blender in batches), blend the mixture until soup is smooth.
11. Return soup to low heat and add additional vegetable broth to reach desired consistency and/or adjust the seasoning with extra salt and pepper.
12. Serve with extra basil and olive oil, and enjoy!

Tip: In the winter months when soup cravings are at a high, I have also made this recipe with whatever tomato I have available. I usually like to add a few orange ones to lighten up the color of the soup, and bring in a variety of antioxidants.

Fresh Spring Pea Soup

This soup will definitely make you feel the promise of spring time. The bright-green color and fresh flavor from the peas will fill your taste buds with light spring delight. This soup is so simple to make, and is an excellent light meal, especially after a winter of eating hearty, and comfort foods. Garnished with fresh-cut chives, thinly sliced leeks, hemp seeds, and a swirl of coconut milk, it looks almost too pretty to eat!

Servings: *5+*	**Prep time:** *10 mins*	**Cook time:** *20 mins*

Ingredients

5 cups frozen peas or if you have fresh ones it's even better

2 cups vegetable stock, low sodium, organic

2 cups filtered water

1 cup chopped green onion

1 cup fresh mint, chopped

⅓ cup fresh parsley, chopped

2 Tbsp extra virgin olive oil

2 tsp sea salt

½ tsp ground black pepper

Directions

1. In a large saucepan, add the olive oil and onion, cook over medium-low heat for 5–10 minutes, until softened.
2. Add the vegetable stock and water, and increase the heat to allow the mixture to come to a boil.
3. Add the peas and cook for 2–3 minutes (very quick cooking), until the peas are tender. If you're using fresh peas, it will take 4–5 minutes.
4. Taking the pot off the heat, add in fresh herbs, salt, pepper, and adjust for seasonings.
5. Next, pour half of the mixture into the blender (or divide the mixture in thirds) and puree/blend a little at a time until the entire mixture is creamy.
6. Garnish with fresh cut chives, pumpkin seeds, hemp seeds, or pea shoots.

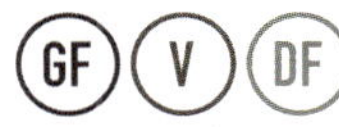

Spiced Carrot-Turmeric Soup

This spiced carrot and turmeric soup screams fall coziness. I especially love this soup when the local, organic carrots are freshly harvested as they have such a sweet, crispness. Turmeric with its bright orange and earthy flavor is a beautiful complement to the sweetness of carrots.

Servings: *4*	**Prep time:** *15 mins*	**Cook time:** *10 mins*

Ingredients

12 medium-sized carrots, peeled and sliced

2 Tbsp olive oil

1 medium onion, chopped

3 cloves of garlic, chopped

1 Tbsp fresh ginger, grated

1 tsp fresh turmeric, grated
(or turmeric powder)

½ tsp black pepper

½ tsp salt

4 cups vegetable broth

Directions

1. Sauté the onions over medium heat in a pan with 2 tablespoons of olive oil. Once they're translucent and soft, add the garlic, ginger, turmeric, carrots, and seasoning.
2. Sauté everything for another 2–3 minutes over medium heat.
3. Add the hot vegetable stock, bring to a boil, and simmer for 5 minutes.
4. Puree the soup in your high-speed blender.
5. Serve with some toasted pumpkin seeds, red pepper flakes, or on its own.

Hearty Black-Eyed Pea Kale Soup

A hearty, veggie-loaded soup with earthy root vegetables and carrots is one of the most comforting and delicious foods to enjoy during the cool fall and winter months. This soup is easy to prepare, loaded with flavor, and very nourishing. I make this soup during the week and/or for a rainy Saturday lunch especially after the boys have been playing soccer outside. It's soup that feels good, like a big hug.

Servings: *6–8*	**Prep time:** *15 mins*	**Cook time:** *25 mins*

Ingredients

1 leek, cut half, cleaned well, and cut into thin slices

2 cups canned black-eyed peas (or other beans such as white, black, or pinto beans also work), drain and rinse the beans well

8 cups vegetable stock

2 cups organic kale, chopped

6 large carrots, chopped

2 stalks of celery, thinly sliced

2 small turnips, peeled and cut into medium pieces

2 cloves garlic, minced

2 Tbsp organic coconut oil

1 tsp dried rosemary

1 tsp dried sage

1 tsp cumin

1 tsp sea salt

Pinch of red pepper flakes

Optional – ¼ lb parmesan cheese rind. I love the flavor the rind imparts in the soup. Simply add it to the broth and let it cook. Remove when ready to serve.

Optional – If you like the flavor of a tomato-based soup, add 1 can of crushed tomatoes to the broth.

Directions

1. In a saucepan on medium heat, add coconut oil and leeks and cook until softened. Add in celery, carrots, turnips, and garlic and cook until the mixture is soft and caramelized.
2. Add spices, salt, and pepper to this mixture.
3. In a large pot, pour in vegetable stock and beans.
4. Add the sautéed mixture and cook over a low simmer until flavors are incorporated and beans are soft (about 20 minutes). Don't overcook the vegetables.
5. When soup is ready, add kale at the end and cook until it's wilted. Don't overcook the kale.
6. Stir occasionally and adjust the flavor to your taste.

Corn Chowder

This corn chowder is rich and hearty without all the cream and butter found in most chowders. I love this one served with a warmed up crusty loaf of sourdough bread (especially good when dipped in the chowder).

Servings: *5–6*	**Prep time:** *10 mins*	**Cook time:** *30 mins*

Ingredients

1 large yellow onion, diced

3 garlic cloves, chopped

¼ cup extra virgin olive oil

4 cups sweet corn (fresh, frozen, or canned)

3 cups chopped russet potatoes

1 medium red pepper, diced

3 cups vegetable stock

¼ cup almond flour

¼ cup almond milk

3 Tbsp full-fat coconut milk

1 tsp salt

½ tsp black pepper

¼ tsp cayenne pepper

Directions

1. In a large pot, heat the olive oil on medium and sauté the onion until it's translucent.
2. Add the chopped garlic, salt, pepper, cayenne, potatoes, red peppers, and vegetable stock. Bring to a boil over medium heat. Reduce the heat and simmer until the potatoes are soft, for about 15 minutes.
3. Add the corn at this point and cook for another 10 minutes.
4. Steam the almond milk and transfer it to a blender along with the coconut milk and the almond flour. Set aside!
5. Transfer 3 cups of the soup in to the same blender and blend until smooth. Transfer it back to the pot along with the almond flour mixture.
6. Adjust the taste by adding more salt or pepper.
7. Serve warm and garnish with extra cooked corn.

Hearty Minestrone Soup

Make it a minestrone kinda night with this soup that eats like a meal. There are endless combinations of vegetables that you can use in a minestrone. In the spring, try asparagus and peas, in the fall beans, carrots, sweet potatoes, etc. You can keep it vegetarian, or add your favorite meatballs.

Servings: *6*	**Prep time:** *15 mins*	**Cook time:** *30 mins*

Ingredients

4 Tbsp extra virgin olive oil

4 garlic cloves, minced

4 large carrots, diced

2 cups green beans, trimmed and cut into ½-inch pieces

2 cups white cabbage, shredded

6 cups low-sodium vegetable broth

1 large can (14 oz) organic diced tomato

1½ cups fusilli pasta (or your favorite pasta)

1 can navy or cannellini beans

1 Tbsp dried oregano

1 Tbsp dried basil

½ tsp chili flakes

1 tsp sea salt

¼ tsp fresh black pepper

Fresh basil and parmesan cheese for topping (optional)

Directions

1. In a large pot, heat the olive oil over medium heat. Add the onion and sauté for 3 minutes until it's translucent. Add the garlic and cook for another minute.
2. Add the carrots and cook until they begin to soften, about 5 minutes.
3. Stir in the green beans, cabbage, oregano, basil, chili flakes, sea salt, black pepper, diced tomatoes, and vegetable broth.
4. Bring to a boil, then reduce heat to medium-low and simmer for 10 minutes.
5. Stir in the pasta and beans and cook until pasta is tender about 10 minutes. Adjust the seasoning before serving.
6. Serve and top with fresh basil or parmesan.

Vegan Cream of Mushroom Soup

Creamy fungi heaven in a bowl. This soup combines the hearty, earthy nutrition of mushrooms, along with complete creamy deliciousness from the full-fat coconut milk. This is such a great weeknight soup. I love serving it with toasted sourdough bread for dipping.

Servings: *4*	**Prep time:** *15 mins*	**Cook time:** *15 mins*

Ingredients

4 Tbsp olive oil

1 medium onion, chopped

¼ cup shallots, sliced

2 medium garlic cloves, minced

4 Tbsp olive oil

6 cups sliced cremini mushrooms

1 tsp sea salt

½ tsp black pepper

1 tsp dried thyme

4 Tbsp arrow root flour

2 cups vegetable broth, low sodium

1½ cup full-fat coconut milk, canned coconut milk works best

Directions

1. In a medium pot, heat the olive oil on medium heat. Add in the onions, shallots, and cook until it's soft and golden, for about 4 minutes.
2. Add in the garlic and cook for another minute. Next add the mushrooms and spices (salt, pepper, thyme). Cook for 5 minutes until the mushrooms have softened.
3. Stir in the arrow root starch and make sure that it is completely dissolved and mixed in before adding the liquids.
4. Add the vegetable broth and coconut milk while stirring frequently.
5. Cook on high heat for 3 minutes until the soup has slightly thickened.
6. Serve hot with a slice of bread or as a side dish. Enjoy!
7. Leftover can be refrigerated for up to 3 days.

Tomato Lentil Soup

The combination of lentils and spices such as cumin and curry give this soup a cozy grounding feel that I especially love throughout the fall and winter months. Lentils are always one of my favorite legumes to use, and this has been a well-loved soup in our home for many years.

Servings: *5+*	**Prep time:** *15 mins*	**Cook time:** *30 mins*

Ingredients

2 Tbsp extra virgin olive oil

2 medium yellow onions, chopped

3 carrots, cleaned and sliced

4 garlic cloves, minced

2 tsp ground cumin

1 tsp curry powder

2 cups red lentils, soaked for 3 hours (or if you don't have time to soak them, just cook the soup a little longer)

1 can (28 oz) diced tomates

4 cups vegetable broth

1 tsp salt

Pinch of cayenne pepper

Freshly ground black pepper

2 cups chopped fresh kale (or baby spinach leaves)

Directions

1. In a large pot, heat the olive oil over medium. Once the oil is heated add the onion and carrot. Cook for about 5 minutes, or until the onion has softened.
2. Add garlic, cumin, and curry powder. Cook until fragrant, while stirring constantly (about 1 minute).
3. Add the remaining ingredients, except chopped kale (lentils, tomatoes, vegetable broth, salt, cayenne pepper, black pepper).
4. Bring the mixture to a boil, then reduce the heat and partially cover with the lid.
5. Allow to cook for 30–40 minutes or until the lentils are soft.
6. Remove the pot from the heat and stir in the chopped kale.
7. Serve immediately. Leftovers can be refrigerated for up to a week.
8. Enjoy!

Tip: Soaking the lentils will make them easier to digest, and easier to cook.

Cauliflower Turmeric Soup

When cauliflower and turmeric meet, the result is a creamy, fragrant, and delicious soup that can be ready in 30 minutes with just 5 simple ingredients. Turmeric is arguably one of the healthiest spices, and every chance I get to include it in my diet, I go for it. I love it with fish, curry, golden milk, and smoothies. The possibilities are endless.

Servings: *4*	**Prep time:** *15 mins*	**Cook time:** *1 h + cooling*

Ingredients

1 medium cauliflower

2 Tbsp coconut oil

3 cups boiling water

1 cup full-fat coconut milk

2 pinch fresh turmeric

Salt and pepper to taste

Directions

1. Preheat the oven to 400 °F (205 °C).
2. Cut the cauliflower head into florets.
3. Coat the cauliflower florets with coconut oil. On a baking sheet, cook the cauliflower for 20 minutes or until they are soft and golden, tossing them half way through.
4. Transfer the cooled cauliflower into a high-speed blender.
5. Add the hot water, coconut milk, turmeric, salt, and pepper into the blender.
6. Blend on high until the mixture forms a creamy texture.
7. You can add more hot water or coconut milk to thin it.
8. Adjust the flavor to your taste. Top off with pumpkin seeds, sesame seeds, or a few slices of avocado. Serve and enjoy!
9. This creamy soup can be served hot or at room temperature.

Green Goddess Soup

You will glow and feel like a goddess with this delicious, creamy, and fresh green goddess soup. Leeks are a great cleansing vegetable and I use them in a lot of cooking in place of onions, especially in the spring months. You could choose to leave this soup whole rather than pureeing, but with my kids sometimes picking out the veggies they don't love, it's often easier to puree. Either way, this soup is a favorite!

Servings: *4*	**Prep time:** *20 mins*	**Cook time:** *30 mins*

Ingredients

4 Tbsp extra virgin olive oil

2 leeks, cleaned and thinly sliced

4 garlic, thinly sliced

3 medium white potatoes, peeled and cubed

2 medium zucchini

1 cup packed kales leaves, stems removed

2 cups packed spinach

¼ cup parsley, chopped

1 cup vegetable stock

1½ cup canned coconut milk

1 tsp sea salt

½ tsp black pepper

Pinch of chili flakes

Directions

1. In a deep saucepan, heat olive oil and leeks over medium heat and sauté for 10 minutes.
2. Add the garlic, zucchini, and potatoes and cook for another 5 minutes stirring frequently.
3. Add 1 cup of vegetable stock and cover with the lid. Let the potatoes cook thoroughly for another 15 minutes.
4. Add kale, spinach, parsley, salt, and chili flakes and remove from the heat. The leafy greens will cook with the steam.
5. Transfer to a high-speed blender; add the coconut milk and blend until smooth. Adjust taste before serving. It's delicious hot or cold!

LIBECO

Lemony Lentil Soup

Lentils are my favorite legume, and make an appearance in many meals in our home; from red lentil pasta, soups, and salads, there are so many versatile ways to use this hearty pulse. I buy dried red lentils in bulk as they keep for a long time and it's a more affordable way to purchase dried goods. If you're making this soup on the stovetop rather than slow cooker, you can soak the lentils ahead of time to speed up the cooking.

Servings: *6*	**Prep time:** *15 mins*	**Cook time:** *2–5 h**

Ingredients

1 Tbsp grapeseed oil or avocado oil

1 brown onion, peeled and diced

3 medium carrots, well washed and diced

5 garlic cloves, minced

6 cups unsalted vegetable stock or chicken broth

1½ cups red lentils, rinsed

⅔ cups frozen corn kernels

2 tsp ground cumin

1 tsp curry powder

¼ tsp ground turmeric (optional)

1 lemon

1 tsp sea salt

½ tsp ground black pepper

Directions

1. Add oil to a frying pan and warm over medium-high heat. Stir in onions and carrots and sauté until vegetables have softened, about 5 minutes.
2. Add garlic and continue to sauté for another minute.
3. Transfer onion mixture to a 5 L or 6 L slow cooker along with stock, lentils, corn, cumin, curry and turmeric, if using.
4. Cover and cook on high for 2–3 hours, or on low for 5–6 hours, until lentils are completely tender. You can leave it whole or puree it by using an immersion blender to desired consistency. In a blender, you will need to puree the soup in batches.
5. Return soup to slow cooker and stir in half a lemon's worth of zest, one whole lemon's worth of juice, salt, and pepper. Serve warm.
6. Soup may be made ahead of time and refrigerated in an airtight container for up to 3 days or frozen for up to 3 months.

Tip: To add an extra kick of protein, place a chicken breast or two in the slow cooker along with other ingredients and cook as directed. Remove chicken breast before pureeing soup, shred using a pair of forks and stir back into finished soup.

*Depending on your setting on slow cooker.

Slow Cooker Tortilla Soup

Slow cookers are genius. Period. A little bit of prep in the morning before you leave for the day, and you will walk into your house hours later with the aroma of a home-cooked dinner welcoming you in. How great is that? I use my slow cookers on days when I know we've got multiple after-school and or evening commitments with very little time in between. The sweet, spicy, and savory taste of this soup will add a little fiesta to your dinner.

Servings: *4*	**Prep time:** *15 mins*	**Cook time:** *40 mins*

Ingredients

½ lb boneless and skinless chicken breast (about 1 large breast)

½ lb boneless and skinless chicken thighs (about 2–3 thighs)

1 can (28 oz) diced tomatoes, do not drain

1 can (14 oz) black beans, drained

1 cup frozen corn kernels

½ medium red onion, diced

3 garlic cloves, minced

3 cups unsalted chicken broth

1 tsp salt, plus extra for seasoning tortilla crisps

1½ tsp ground cumin

1 tsp chili powder

¼ tsp cayenne pepper (optional)

¼ tsp smoked paprika (optional)

1 tsp dried oregano

Juice of 1 lime

2 Tbsp cilantro leaves, chopped

5 corn tortillas

3 Tbsp grapeseed oil or avocado oil, plus extra

1 avocado, cut into chunks

½ cup sour cream or plain Greek yogurt

Directions

1. Lay chicken breast and thighs in bottom of a 5 L or 6 L slow cooker. Top with roasted tomatoes, black beans, corn, onion, garlic, chicken broth, salt, ground cumin, chili powder, cayenne (if using), smoked paprika (if using), oregano, lime juice, and cilantro. Take two tortillas, cut or tear into strips and add to slow cooker. Cover and cook on high for 3–4 hours, or on low for 5–6 hours, until chicken is tender.
2. Remove chicken and dice or shred. Stir back into soup.
3. Heat oil in a large frying pan over medium-high heat. Slice remaining 3 tortillas into long thin strips. In batches, adding more oil as necessary, fry tortilla strips until golden brown and crisp, about 3–4 minutes. Transfer to a paper towel-lined plate to drain and season with a light sprinkling of salt, if desired.
4. Divide soup among serving bowls and top with some avocado, a dollop of sour cream or yogurt, and some tortilla crisps. Enjoy while warm.

Tip: Set out a buffet style with all the topping options from shredded cheese (I love crumbled cojita on top of this soup), green onion, cilantro, avocado, sour cream, or yogurt, jalapeños, and tortillas and let everyone help themselves.

Roasted Butternut Squash Soup

Creamy, sweet, savory, and oh so cozy, this roasted butternut squash is a delicious and easy fall classic. Because of its rich and nourishing consistency, it eats as a meal, but also makes a great starter soup before a thanksgiving or fall dinner.

Servings: *4*	**Prep time:** *15 mins*	**Cook time:** *40 mins*

Ingredients

4 cups of cubed butternut squash

2 Tbsp olive oil

½ tsp salt

¼ tsp pepper

3 cups vegetable stock

1 cup full-fat coconut milk

Directions

1. Preheat the oven to 375 °F (190 °C). Line a rimmed baking sheet with parchment paper. Place the butternut squash on the pan and drizzle olive oil to lightly coat the squash. Sprinkle with salt and pepper.
2. Bake for 40 minutes or until the squash is soft and lightly golden.
3. Allow to cool down for a few minutes before transferring to your high-speed blender along with the vegetable stock and coconut milk.
4. Blend on high until the texture is creamy. At this point you can adjust the seasoning and if you would like to thin out the soup you can always add ¼ cup of coconut milk at a time and re-blend.
5. Serve immediately, or reheat at a later time if you like your soup on the warmer side. Top with a drizzle of coconut milk, sesame seeds, or chili flakes.

VEGGIES

In case you haven't heard, vegetables are cool! Eating vegetables is cost-effective, they are delicious, great for digestion, and above all, they keep you fit and healthy. There are hundreds of ways to enjoy them, roasted, baked, boiled, or buried in a cream sauce; you can even spiralize your favorite vegetables to make them look and taste just like pasta! Have you ever prepared garbanzo bean pasta? If not, you don't know what you're missing!

Over the years there has been a shift towards eating more plants and less animal foods. Research shows a plant-based diet is healthier and better for our planet. The fastest food in the world is raw food; therefore some of the most affordable and straightforward meals center on raw, natural food. A salad can be chopped and made into a protein-rich meal by merely adding delicious and nutritious plant-based toppings such as hemp seeds, pepitas, or garbanzo beans.

Making vegetables taste delicious has been an area of focus in my role as a mom to my three kids. Feeding and introducing healthy food to three children under the age of ten is not easy. My son Matteo is a self-reported carnivore, and he proclaims "I don't like veggies!" However, he actually likes them more than he realizes and when I place a bowl of freshly steamed broccoli drizzled in olive oil with a pinch of sea salt, he grabs into the bowl and eats them like candy. My kids tend to enjoy the simple veggies such as broccoli, carrots, cucumbers, and bell peppers. When I introduce new vegetables, it's not always met with as much enthusiasm as I would like. However, I keep trying knowing that it may take more than one introduction of any new food, or spice to get my kids to accept and enjoy them. Our vegetable repertoire has expanded over the last ten years, and I'm proud to say that my kids will try and eat almost every food.

As I mentioned earlier, spiralizing has to be one of the most fun ways to prepare vegetables for kids. It is a great way to get your family to swap out a grain-based pasta in favor of a veggie-based one. A simple, hand-held spiralizer is a great tool to have on hand. Zucchini and squash can be spiralized with this tool; more fibrous vegetables such as beets and sweet potato may require a more robust attachment. I have prepared lots of delicious, nourishing plant-based sauces that can be swirled into your favorite spiralized vegetable, or poured on top after they are roasted or steamed. My kids gobble them up. These dishes are bright and colorful, and they look like fancy pasta. Once the sauce goes on and perhaps a little cheese, they dive in.

Salads are healthy and a staple item that I highly recommend. With salads they come in endless configurations; they're easy to create. Plus, preparing a fresh salad dressing on the weekend can be a time-saver, so you're ready for all your busy weeknight salads.

I recommend a simple ratio: three parts extra virgin olive oil, one part acid (lemon juice, lime, orange, or your favorite vinegar) and a pinch of sea salt and pepper. You can sweeten any dressing with honey, and to make it extra special, add fresh garlic, Dijon mustard, red pepper flakes, or any of your favorite herbs. Put all the ingredients in a mason jar, shake, and store until ready to serve. Salad dressing will last 3 days.

I hope this chapter inspires you to experiment and make veggies a more significant part of your families' dinner plate.

Spiralized Zucchini

As you can see throughout this book, I provide a lot of sauce and dip options. These can all be used with your favorite pasta or spiralized vegetables or with crackers, bread, or chips. My favorite veggies to spiralize include zucchini, butternut squash, sweet potatoes, and beets. I highly recommend investing in a small, hand-held spiralizer that can easily spiralize zucchini – it takes under 5 minutes.

Servings: *2**	**Prep time:** *less than 5 mins*	**Cook time:** *n/a*

Ingredients

Zucchini
*Medium sized

Directions

1. The easiest way to cook spiralized zucchini is to simply sauté it in olive oil, fresh garlic, and a pinch of sea salt and pepper.
2. Swirl through your favorite sauce or enjoy as a side dish. Either way, being healthy has never been easier.

Tip: If you plan to spiralize more of the fibrous root veggies, you may want to buy a more robust spiralizer or it can be found as an attachment for stand mixers.

Artichokes

Artichokes have to be one of the most beautiful vegetables in the world. I had never eaten an artichoke until I married into an Italian family, and let's just say, they love their marinated artichokes. And as soon as I got past the intimidation factor, artichokes soon became one of my favorites that we love to serve as part of a charcuterie platter, or "condiment" at a BBQ. Artichokes and can be baked, grilled, boiled, steamed, stuffed, and marinated.

Servings: *2*	**Prep time:** *10 mins*	**Cook time:** *35 mins*

Ingredients

2 fresh artichokes, peel the outer leaves closest to the stem; trim the remaining prickly "tops" with scissors so they are flat in shape

½ lemon

½ tsp salt

1 garlic clove

Olive oil/balsamic dip

- ¼ cup extra virgin olive oil
- 2 Tbsp aged balsamic vinegar
- Pinch of black pepper and salt to taste
- Whisk in a small bowl

While I was writing this chapter, my friend's mother-in-law, who is almost 90 years old, filmed a short video on how she makes her delicious artichokes that her grandchildren absolutely love; and in true "nona" style, it was a little of this and a little of that. It brought tears to my eyes and I will forever cherish this video she made for me.

Directions for steaming

1. Fill a large pot with water. Add about 1 tsp of salt, ½ lemon, 1 garlic clove. Add a steaming basket to the pot. Bring to a boil.
2. Meanwhile, prepare artichokes by cutting the top off and then peeling tough outer leaves (this part is not edible). Also with scissors trim the pointy/prickly top of the leaf so that it's flat. This will make the artichoke easier to handle and eat. Once trimmed, run artichokes under cold water.
3. Add artichokes to steam basket and return to a low boil.
4. Continue steaming for 30–40 minutes or until you can gently pull a leaf from the center of the artichoke.
5. Once cooked, remove from pot. Let cool slightly (they actually taste delicious warm then dipped in the olive oil mixture). Pull the inner leaves out and trim off the tough outer part, or if you want your teeth to do a little more of the work you can dip the leaf into an olive oil/vinegar mixture or your favorite sauce then draw the base of the artichoke leaf through your teeth to reveal the soft and delicious inside. Throw away the exterior part.
6. Also at the base of the choke is the "heart". You need to scrape away the tough fuzzy inedible part to reveal the beautiful heart. You can marinade this part as well or use the same dip. The hearts are often canned/jarred and are a delicious topping on a salad.

Tip: The edible part of an artichoke is at the base of the petal, so be sure to remove those tough outer leaves.

Corn & Black Bean Salsa

This corn and black bean salsa makes the perfect side salad, topping for your fajitas or tacos, and can even be served on top of a bed of greens. No matter what way you decide to enjoy, this salsa will add a little fiesta to your dinner.

Servings: *4–6*	**Prep time:** *15 mins*	**Cook time:** *n/a*

Ingredients

2 cups sweet corn (fresh, frozen, or canned)

¼ medium red onion, roughly chopped

1 can of black beans

1 tsp smoked paprika

1 garlic clove minced

1 small bunch of cilantro (remove stem and chop)

¼ tsp sea salt

Cracked pepper to taste

Lime dressing

Juice of 2 limes

1 Tbsp raw honey (liquid/runny kind)

Directions

1. Boil or grill corn on the cob. When cool enough to touch remove kernels from the cob in large pieces (the rougher the texture the better it looks.
2. In a large bowl, add corn, red onion, rinsed black beans, cilantro, and spices.
3. In a small bowl, whisk dressing ingredients and toss in salad.
4. Serve as a side dish, or on top of a bed of mixed greens.

Orange Beet Kale Salad

This salad is wonderfully versatile. Serve it on its own or with simply grilled fish, chicken, or beef. Try changing up the flavors by using grapefruit, dried cherries, and almonds instead of beets, oranges, and hazelnuts.

Servings: *4–6*	**Prep time:** *25 mins*	**Cook time:** *n/a*

Ingredients

2 medium beets, peeled

1 bunch fresh kale, washed and dried

2 Tbsp extra virgin olive oil

2 Tbsp lemon juice

½ tsp lemon zest

2 large navel orange

1 cup packed baby arugula leaves, washed and dried

⅓ cup feta cheese, crumbled

⅓ cup toasted hazelnuts or pecans, coarsely chopped

Salt and freshly ground black pepper to taste

Directions

1. In a small saucepan, place a steamer basket. Fill saucepan with water to just below the steamer basket. Bring to a boil. Cut beets in half and steam until tender, about 10–15 minutes. Make sure to check periodically that the water has not all evaporated. Remove beets from steamer, let cool to room temperature and chop into ½-inch pieces.
2. Meanwhile, trim kale and remove stalks. Stack kale leaves one on top of the other and slice into ribbons. Place kale ribbons in a large bowl and drizzle with olive oil, lemon juice, lemon zest, and a good pinch of salt.
3. Massage kale with your hands until it begins to soften and wilt. Set kale aside to marinate for 10 minutes.
4. Cut away peel from oranges and slice into segments by cutting on either side of the thin white membrane, separating each segment.
5. When ready to serve, toss orange segments, beets, and arugula with the kale. Season to taste with salt and pepper and divide among serving plates.
6. Garnish with feta cheese and hazelnuts.

Hearty Rainbow Salad

My favorite lunch is a hearty salad that eats like a meal. For me that requires protein, healthy fats, and fiber. This salad hits the spot and is so refreshing and flavorful. I also love to place a spoonful of hummus or avocado on top for extra creaminess.

Servings: *2*	**Prep time:** *25 mins*	**Cook time:** *n/a*

Ingredients

Salad

- 1 medium iceberg lettuce, leaves removed and washed
- 1 cup cherry tomatoes, halved
- 5 radishes, thinly sliced
- 1 medium English cucumber, sliced
- 2 medium carrots, made into ribbons
- 2 cup sauté mushrooms, any kind of mushrooms works
- 1 can of black-eyed peas, drained and rinsed

Dressing

- ¼ cup extra virgin olive oil
- Juice of 1 medium lemon
- 3 Tbsp apple cider vinegar
- 1 tsp raw honey
- 1 tsp dried oregano
- Salt and pepper to taste

Directions

1. Add all the salad dressing ingredients into a mason jar. Shake well and set aside.
2. Prepare the salad by assembling the iceberg lettuce leaves on a large salad plate, followed by the remaining ingredients. Drizzle the dressing over the salad and toss to mix.
3. Serve right away!

Creamy Vegan Caesar Dressing

Caesar salad is such a delicious salad dressing option. I love serving it on top of a combination of crunchy romaine and kale leaves. Most Caesar salad dressings are very high in calories and not so healthy fats, but my vegan Caesar dressing made from cashew and hummus is so delicious and packs a ton of protein and good fats into your salad. This one eats like a meal.

Servings: *6–8*	**Prep time:** *10 mins*	**Cook time:** *n/a*

Ingredients

1 cup raw unsalted cashews, soaked for 2 hours

4 Tbsp hummus, preferably one with garlic flavor (I like *Habibi's* hummus)

1 clove of garlic, minced

Juice of 1 lemon

¾ cup water

¼ tsp paprika

¼ tsp black pepper

Pinch of cayenne pepper

Sea salt to taste

Directions

1. Blend all the ingredients in a blender or a food processor until smooth and creamy.
2. Serve over your salad of any combination for an even better taste.
3. Keep the leftovers in an airtight container for up to a week.

Traditional Caesar Dressing

And if you like the traditional dressing made with mayo, this one is the BEST. I've shared this recipe with so many people, and it's a favorite amongst friends and family.

Servings: *6–8*	**Prep time:** *10 mins*	**Cook time:** *n/a*

Ingredients

½ cup extra virgin olive oil

2 Tbsp mayo

1 Tbsp Worcestershire sauce

½ lemon, squeezed

½ tsp salt

Cracked pepper to taste

3 Tbsp parmesan cheese, grated

1 garlic clove, minced

Directions

1. Add all ingredients to a mason jar or resealable container. Shake and refrigerate for a minimum of 3 hours.
2. Let sit at room temp for about 15 minutes before serving.

Avocado Dressing

Avocados are one of the most versatile and creamy foods that make such a delicious base for salad dressing. Smooth, tangy, and full of skin-loving healthy fats, this dressing will become a favorite that you will make every week.

Servings: *2*	**Prep time:** *5 mins*	**Cook time:** *n/a*

Ingredients

2 ripe avocadoes, pitted and skin removed

⅓ cup olive oil

⅓ cup filtered water

Juice of 1 medium lemon

2 small garlic cloves

½ tsp sea salt

Pinch of black pepper

Directions

1. Add all the ingredients in a food processor or blender. Blend until it's smooth and has a creamy texture.
2. To thin it out you can add 1 tablespoon of water at a time.
3. Serve with your favorite green salad.
4. Any leftover can be refrigerated in an airtight container for up to 3 days.

Strawberry, Fennel Salad & Lemony Chia Dressing

This fresh salad screams spring and summer. This is a class recipe that I have made, changed, tweaked, and loved over the years. Each component of this salad is delicious, especially when topped with the healthy lemony chia dressing. Most of these sweet salad dressings are loaded with sugar, but you can feel good about this one as its not overly sweet, and uses honey as the natural sweetener.

Servings: *4–6*	**Prep time:** *15 mins*	**Cook time:** *n/a*

Ingredients

6 cups of your favorite greens.
I like a combination of head of red leaf lettuce, baby spinach, and spring mix

1 fennel bulb, peeled and sliced into long strips

½ medium red onion, thinly sliced

2 cups of fresh strawberries, washed, hulled, and sliced (you could also add blueberries or raspberries)

¼ cup of goat cheese, crumbled

½ avocado, cubed

Optional candied walnuts or pecans (simply toss with maple syrup and roast in oven until crispy and fragrant).

Lemony chia dressing

¼ cup olive oil

2 Tbsp lemon juice

2 Tbsp white balsamic vinegar

2 tsp honey

2 tsp chia seeds

Pinch of salt and black pepper to taste

Directions

1. Add all dressing ingredients to a mason jar. Shake well and set aside.
2. Prepare salad by placing your greens in a large salad bowl. Layer all other ingredients on top of greens. (Add the avocado last and after you've tossed in the dressing).
3. Pour dressing and toss just before serving.

Tip: There are so many options for the type of greens, fruit, cheese, and nuts used. This one is always a crowd pleaser.

Massaged Kale Salad with Dijon-Lemon Dressing

Kale is one of the most nutritious greens to eat; and can be used in so many dishes from soups, pastas, curries, and of course as a base for salads. I love massaging the leaves with a little olive oil to help soften them and make them easier to eat. This is kale salad perfection!

Servings: *4*	**Prep time:** *15 mins*	**Cook time:** *n/a*

Ingredients

Dijon-lemon dressing

- Juice of 2 lemons
- ¼ cup olive oil
- 4 Tbsp Dijon mustard
- 1 clove of garlic, minced
- 1 Tbsp raw honey
- ½ tsp salt
- ¼ tsp fresh ground pepper

Massaged kale salad

- 2 bunch dinosaur kale
- ¼ cup chopped hazelnuts (or any nut)
- 3 large carrots, julienned
- Baked sweet potatoes (optional)

Directions

1. Combine all the ingredients for the dressing in a blender. Adjust the taste by adding more salt, pepper, or honey.
2. Wash and dry the kale leaves. Stipe leaves from the stems. Tear them in small pieces and place them in a large bowl. Drizzle a little olive oil and lightly massage the kale. This helps soften it and makes it easier to digest.
3. Add the remaining ingredients (hazelnuts, carrots, sweet potatoes). Drizzle the dressing on top and toss.
4. Enjoy by adding a side of protein to it such as (quinoa, baked chicken, fish), or enjoy it on its own with a dollop of.hummus.

Zucchini Summer Pasta

A spiralizer is one of the best kitchen gadgets around. It allows you to easily transform some of your favorite veggies into salads or "zoodles" (zucchini noodles). Zoodles make a satisfying, refreshing, and nutritious swap for pasta – in fact they are so delicious that I would prefer a zoodle over a noodle. You could also spiralizer butternut squash or sweet potatoes for this recipe.

Servings: *4*	**Prep time:** *10 mins*	**Cook time:** *35 mins*

Ingredients

2 cups baby tomatoes, cut in halves

4 medium zucchinis

1½ cup fresh corn, removed from the cob (may also use frozen)

1 sweet onion, diced

3 Tbsp olive oil

½ tsp salt

¼ tsp freshly ground black pepper

¼ tsp red pepper flakes

¼ cup chopped parsley, to garnish

Parmesan cheese, to garnish

Directions

1. Preheat oven to 350 °F (175 °C).
2. Place the tomatoes on a baking sheet and roast for 30 minutes.
3. While the tomatoes are roasting, using a spiralizer, spiralize zucchinis into noodle shape.
4. In a frying pan sauté the onion with olive oil until golden brown (medium heat). Add the fresh corn, black pepper, salt, red pepper flakes, and cook for another 10 minutes.
5. Add the zucchini noodle and cook for another 3 minutes.
6. Adjust the seasoning if needed.
7. When ready to serve, top it off with the roasted tomatoes, parsley, and Parmesan cheese.
8. For lean protein options, add baked chicken breast, cooked garbanzo beans, or a dollop of hummus. Options are unlimited!

Mediterranean Quinoa Salad

This fresh and hearty salad will steal the show at your next dinner. Try serving it alongside simply grilled or baked fish or topped with slices of roasted chicken.

Servings: *4*	**Prep time:** *20 mins*	**Cook time:** *n/a*

Ingredients

¾ cup quinoa

1½ cup water

1 cup diced avocado

1 cup cherry tomatoes, cut in half

½ cup frozen green peas, thawed

1 cup red bell pepper, diced

½ cup yellow bell pepper, diced

⅓ cup red onion, diced

1 cup mini bocconcini cheese, cut in half (optional)

3 Tbsp balsamic vinegar

2 Tbsp extra virgin olive oil

2 Tbsp Dijon mustard

2 Tbsp chopped fresh oregano (or 2 tsp dried oregano)

2 Tbsp chopped fresh parsley

1 garlic clove, minced

Salt and black pepper, to taste

Directions

1. In a saucepan, bring quinoa and water to a boil over high heat. Reduce heat to medium-low, cover, and simmer for 10 minutes. Turn the heat off, keeping saucepan covered and on the burner, allowing the residual heat to continue cooking quinoa until all the liquid has been absorbed, about 4 minutes. If there's still a little bit of water that has not been absorbed, leave the saucepan covered on the burner for another 3–5 minutes.
2. Meanwhile, in a large bowl, stir together avocado, tomatoes, peas, red and yellow peppers, onion, and bocconcini to combine.
3. In another bowl, whisk together vinegar, olive oil, mustard, oregano, parsley and garlic. Season to taste with salt and pepper. Pour vinaigrette over vegetables and add quinoa. Stir lightly until everything is well combined. Season with salt and pepper to your taste.
4. This salad keeps well, stored in the refrigerator for 3 days.

Cucumber Noodle Salad

The ultimate in freshness, cucumbers have one of the highest water content of any vegetable, and are so hydrating and detoxifying for the body. This salad is honestly one of the freshest I have ever created. And if you haven't tried Greek haloumi cheese before, well you are in for a treat.

Servings: *4*	**Prep time:** *20 mins*	**Cook time:** *n/a*

Ingredients

5 Lebanese cucumbers, divided (or 2 English cucumbers)

1 cup fresh basil leaves, divided

½ cup cashews

¼ cup fresh parsley leaves

2 Tbsp chopped chives

½ tsp salt

1 Tbsp extra virgin olive oil

¼ cup water

1 tsp grapeseed oil

½ cup frozen corn kernels

½ lb haloumi cheese, cut into 4 slices

1½ cups cherry tomatoes, cut in half

½ cup pitted Kalamata olives, halved

Freshly ground black pepper, for garnish

Directions

1. Start by making the salad dressing. In a blender, combine 1 roughly chopped cucumber with ½ cup basil leaves, cashews, oregano, chives, salt, olive oil and water until smooth. Taste for seasoning and adjust with additional salt if desired. Set aside.
2. Using a spiralizer or vegetable peeler, cut remaining 4 cucumbers into thin noodles and place into a large bowl. Set aside.
3. Heat oil in a nonstick frying pan over medium heat. Add corn and sauté until starting to brown, about 4 minutes. Remove corn to a plate and place frying pan back over heat.
4. Add haloumi cheese slices to frying pan and cook until golden brown on both sides, about 2 minutes on each side.
5. Tear haloumi into small pieces and place in bowl with cucumber noodles along with corn, tomatoes, olives, remaining ½ cup basil leaves and dressing.
6. Lightly toss to combine. Divide salad between serving bowls and garnish with a sprinkle of freshly ground pepper, if desired.

Tip: For this recipe, you can also use two English cucumbers. Use a third of one cucumber in the dressing and use a spiralizer for the rest of the salad.

Wheat Berry Quinoa Kale Salad

This hearty salad is a spinoff of my favorite salad at *Browns Socialhouse* (it's a favorite lunch spot with friends). It's definitely hearty enough to eat as a complete meal, but you could also add extra protein such as grilled chicken, prawns, or salmon. I also love this salad served to guests on the weekend as the vibrant colors and flavors really impress.

Servings: *4–5*	**Prep time:** *25 mins*	**Cook time:** *n/a*

Ingredients

Salad

- 6 cups kale, chopped
- 1 cup cooked quinoa
- 1½ cup cooked wheat berry
- 1 medium golden beet, thinly slides
- 2 cups Brussels sprouts, cut in halves
- 2 Tbsp olive oil
- ½ cup artichoke, sliced (fresh or canned)
- 1 large avocado, diced
- ¼ cup fresh parmesan cheese, shredded
- Mint and dill, to garnish

Dressing

- ¼ cup apple cider vinegar
- 5 Tbsp Dijon mustard
- ¼ cup olive oil
- 3 Tbsp honey
- ½ tsp salt
- ½ tsp black pepper

Directions

1. Add the chopped kale to a large bowl. Using your hands gently massage the kale with some sea salt to soften.
2. In a frying pan, heat the olive oil on medium heat and sauté the Brussels sprouts for 15 minutes until they are soft inside and crispy on the outside.
3. Add the Brussels sprouts, quinoa, wheat berry, golden beets, and artichoke to your salad bowl.
4. For the dressing, add all the ingredients to a Mason jar and shake until it's well mixed together.
5. Drizzle the dressing on top of the salad and give it good mix. Add the Parmesan cheese and avocado; garnish with fresh mint and dill.
6. Serve at room temperature and enjoy!

Cauliflower Tabouli

A little bit of chopping with a whole lot of crunch and flavor. This recipe is a simple, nourishing and fresh take on a classic Middle Eastern dish swapping grains for cauliflower "rice". This salad is perfect for picnics and gatherings, and it looks gorgeous with all the vibrant colors. This recipe keeps really well and makes for delicious leftovers.

Servings: *4*	**Prep time:** *20 mins*	**Cook time:** *chill for 1 h*

Ingredients

1 small head of cauliflower floret, chopped in a food processor or using a box grater

2 large bunches parsley, finely chopped

2 cups tomatoes, finely diced

1 bunch green onions, finely chopped

1 large cucumber, peeled and finely diced

⅓ cup extra-virgin olive oil

3 Tbsp fresh lemon juice

2 Tbsp fresh mint, finely chopped

½ tsp sea salt, plus more to taste

¼ tsp black pepper

Directions

1. To make the cauliflower rice, place the raw florets into a food processor. Using the S-shaped blade pulse into fine pieces.
2. Transfer this mixture to a large mixing bowl, add all of the remaining ingredients, and toss until well combined. Adjust the seasoning!
3. Refrigerate for at least 1 hour before serving.

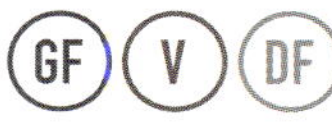

Creamy Coleslaw with Lemon-Tahini Dressing

I love a good "slaw", but I don't like the traditional "mayo"-based dressing... so say hello to the most delicious, smooth, and creamy dressing made with tahini (which is a sesame seed paste). One of the best parts of this salad is it can be made really quickly and easily if you opt to buy your cabbage and carrots already cut. (The premix coleslaw bags are great).

Servings: *4+*	**Prep time:** *20 mins*	**Cook time:** *n/a*

Ingredients

Coleslaw

- 1 head of shredded green cabbage (on a mandolin or thinly sliced with a knife)
- ½ head of shredded purple cabbage (same as above)
- 2 large carrots, julienned or use a carrot peeler to get long curly threads
- 1 red bell pepper, julienned
- 1 scallion, diced
- Toast on a large baking sheet for just a few minutes (be careful to not burn)
- ¼ cup of each coconut flakes, pepitas, and sunflower seeds

Lemon-tahini dressing

- 1½ Tbsp tahini
- 3 Tbsp olive oil
- 1 lemon, juiced
- 2 Tbsp honey
- ½ Tbsp apple cider vinegar
- Pinch of cracked pepper and sea salt
- A splash of water to thin
- Mint leaves or cilantro (optional) – use a high-speed blender to make dressing if using herbs

Directions

Coleslaw

1. Wash the chopped vegetables and add to a large bowl
2. Heat oven to 350 °F (175 °C) and place coconut flakes, pepitas, and sunflower on sheet. Roast for a few minutes. Once cooled, add to the veggies.
3. Pour lemon tahini dressing once ready to serve.

Lemon-tahini dressing

1. Add all ingredients to a mason jar. If adding herbs use a high-speed blender.
2. Shake well. Pour over salad when ready to serve.

Tip: The premix coleslaw bags are great. I also add in extra carrots, julienned bell peppers, coconut flakes, pepitas, sunflower seeds, and voila, a super nourishing bowl of slaw. You could also add diced apples, cucumber, zucchini, raisins, and more. This one will be a huge hit for any family gathering or picnic.

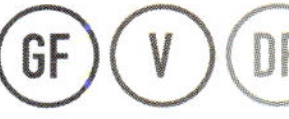

Dill Potato Salad

A summer BBQ classic salad is made so healthy with this light and delicious dill dressing. I love this salad in August and September when fresh baby potatoes are at their peak. There is just something about fresh potatoes that taste so amazing. You could use white, purple or red, or a combination of them makes for an eye-catching salad.

Servings: *4*	**Prep time:** *10 mins*	**Cook time:** *20 mins*

Ingredients

1 lb new potatoes, halved

½ cup fresh dill, chopped

2 scallions, thinly sliced

¼ cup extra virgin olive oil

1 tsp salt

½ tsp black pepper

Directions

1. Fill a large saucepan with 2 inches of water and fit in a steamer basket. Bring the water to a boil. Place the potatoes in the basket, cover, and steam until tender, approximately 20 minutes.
2. Meanwhile, in a medium bowl, mix together the chopped dill, scallion, olive oil, salt, and pepper.
3. Once the potatoes are cooked add them to the bowl and toss to combine.
4. Adjust the seasoning and serve right away!

Coconut-Jalapeño Creamed Corn

We happened to be in Hawaii in August, just as the seasonal set of ingredients used on the menus in one of our favorite restaurants was changing. Served alongside a local fish, was a coconut, jalapeño-creamed corn. It was THE most perfect side dish I have ever eaten, and I knew I wanted to recreate it when we got home. This is my version, and I hope you love it as much as I do.

Servings: *4*	**Prep time:** *10 mins*	**Cook time:** *30 mins*

Ingredients

4 cups sweet corn (fresh, frozen, or canned)

1 can (14 oz) full-fat coconut milk

1 medium jalapeño, sliced into thick rings

1 clove garlic, crushed

1-inch piece of ginger, grated

½ tsp salt

¼ tsp black pepper

Basil for garnish

Directions

1. Shuck the corns, cut off the kernels, and set them aside.
2. Heat the coconut milk in a saucepan over low heat.
3. Add the jalapeño, garlic, and ginger. Increase the heat to bring the coconut milk mixture to a simmer until the flavors come together, about 20 minutes.
4. Remove the jalapeño pieces and garlic from the coconut milk.
5. Add the corn and stir to combine. Simmer for 10 minutes, mixing occasionally, until the corn is cooked. Add in the salt and pepper.
6. When you're ready to serve, garnish with basil.

Creamy Parmesan Brussels Sprouts

If Brussels sprouts conjure up memories of a soggy, flavorless veggie your mother told you to eat, just wait until you try these delicious creamy parmesan Brussels sprouts! Inspired by a recipe I tried years ago from *Chatelaine* magazine, it has become my most requested dish for family gatherings. There are two ways to make the cream sauce one using my *Cashew sauce* (page 215), or the traditional way. Either version tastes delicious.

Servings: *6–8*	**Prep time:** *20 mins*	**Cook time:** *15 mins*

Ingredients

Traditional parmesan cream sauce

¼ cup all-purpose flour

¼ cup butter

1½ cups low-sodium chicken broth

1 cup cream

1 tsp dried thyme

½ tsp salt

2 lb Brussels sprouts

½ cup freshly grated parmesan

2 slices prosciutto cut into thin strips

½ cup toasted pine nuts or slivered almonds

Directions

1. Melt butter in a large saucepan over medium heat. Add flour and stir constantly until bubbly, about 2 minutes. Then, whisking constantly add broth, whipping cream, thyme, and salt. Reduce heat and simmer whisking often, until sauce has thickened enough to coat the back of the spoon from 8–10 minutes.
2. Meanwhile, bring a large pot of water to boil. Remove tough outer leaves and trim stems from sprouts. Cut in half. Cook in boiling water until almost fork-tender, 3–5 minutes. Drain well.
3. Stir sprouts into cream sauce. Cook over medium heat, stirring often until hot, about 3 minutes. Then stir in parmesan. Turn sprouts into a serving bowl and scatter with prosciutto and pine nuts. Taste and add more salt if desired.

Sweet & Spicy Green Beans

My memory of green beans dates back to my childhood and our family garden. In the summer, I would help my mom pick the beans and I would sit in front of the soap operas in the afternoon (we only had 2 channels on TV back then, and of course no "I" anything), trimming and cutting. These sweet and spicy green beans make a flavorful hot side dish perfect for pairing with fish or chicken. If you thought green beans were boring, you must give these a try.

Servings: *4*	**Prep time:** *10 mins*	**Cook time:** *10 mins*

Ingredients

1 lb fresh green beans, washed, ends trimmed, and cut in halves

¼ cup vegetable broth

4 Tbsp tamari sauce

2 Tbsp rice vinegar

2 Tbsp coconut sugar

1 Tbsp olive oil

½ tsp chili flakes

½ tsp sea salt

3 garlic cloves, minced

Thumb-size fresh ginger root, minced

Directions

1. For the sauce, in a small bowl mix together tamari, rice vinegar, coconut sugar, olive oil, chili flakes, and salt; set aside.
2. Heat a large frying pan on medium-to-high heat. Add the beans and vegetable broth. Cover and cook for about 5 minutes until the beans begin to get tender and brighter in color.
3. After 5 minutes remove the lid and continue to cook until the broth has evaporated. Add the ginger and garlic and cook for another 2 minutes while stirring.
4. Add the sauce mixture and let it come to a boil until the sauce thickens – approximately 2–3 minutes.
5. Serve hot as a side dish.

Baked Sweet Potato Fries

As the name implies, sweet potatoes have a delicious sweet and earthy flavor. They are fantastic mashed, mixed with cauliflower, or one of our favorites, made into "fries". You can fry these in a high-heat oil like avocado or grapeseed oil, or simply bake them with coconut oil which brings out even more crispy sweetness! Dip in your favorite sauce or sprinkle with sea salt. They will disappear in minutes!

Servings: *1*	**Prep time:** *15 mins*	**Cook time:** *35 mins*

Ingredients

3 medium sweet potatoes, peeled

2 Tbsp coconut oil

½ tsp salt

¼ tsp pepper

Directions

1 Preheat the oven to 450° F (230 °C). Line your baking sheet with aluminum foil and set aside.

2 Cut the sweet potatoes into sticks. In a large bowl, toss them in olive oil, salt, and pepper.

3 Spread the sweet potato sticks out evenly on the papered baking sheet.

4 Bake until the fries are crisp and golden brown, for about 25–35 minutes.

5 Remove the fries with a spatula and serve with your favorite sauce.

Roasted Butternut Squash

Butternut squash has become a popular vegetable with those trying to eat healthy, thanks to the nutritional benefits of this sweet, yet nutty veggie (similar taste to a pumpkin). It's actually been considered one of the world's healthiest foods and is a rich source of potassium (1 cup has the same amount as a banana), B vitamins, vitamins A and C, magnesium, and fiber.

Servings: *4*	**Prep time:** *10 mins*	**Cook time:** *25 mins*

Ingredients

1 butternut squash cubed

1–2 Tbsp extra virgin olive oil

½ tsp sea salt

Cracked pepper to taste

Other flavor options include:
Garlic, thyme, sage, turmeric, cinnamon (plus a drizzle of maple syrup)

Directions

1. Preheat oven to 400 °F (205 °C).
2. Begin by peeling squash and cubing the flesh.
3. Place in a bowl and add oil, salt, and pepper. Toss to coat.
4. Use a heavy baking sheet lined with parchment paper; lay butternut squash on tray.
5. Bake for about 20–25 minutes turning once during roasting.
6. Serve as a side dish or eat on its own.

Tip: Butternut squash makes a delicious base for soup (see page 145 for my delicious *Roasted Butternut Squash Soup* recipe), as a base for sauces and dips (see page 249), but is equally delicious just simply roasted. Because squash has so much flavor, I usually keep it simple and roast with extra virgin olive oil, sea salt, and cracked pepper.

Maple Turmeric Roasted Rainbow Carrots

I LOVE rainbow carrots. I only wish there were more purple ones in the bag. I can't always find these in the grocery store, but when I do, I always buy them. The taste of the carrot is the same, regardless of the color, so all orange ones will work as well. I love roasting them in their whole, full glory, and letting everyone pick their favorite carrot. These carrots are a staple when cooking for friends and family as they not only taste great, but look very beautiful when served.

Servings: *6+*	**Prep time:** *10 mins*	**Cook time:** *25 mins*

Ingredients

6 large whole carrots, peeled and cut lengthwise in half

1 Tbsp avocado oil

1 Tbsp maple syrup

½ tsp turmeric powder

½ tsp sea salt

Freshly cracked black pepper

Directions

1. Preheat oven to 400 °F (205 °C).
2. Line a baking tray with parchment paper.
3. Prep carrots; lay flat and even on baking tray.
4. In a large Ziploc bag, place carrots along with oil, maple syrup, and spices. Shake until evenly coated.
5. Transfer carrots to baking tray.
6. Bake until fork-tender. Turning a couple times during the process.
7. Serve on a platter.

Roasted Cauliflower with Hemp Seeds

You will be eating these cauliflower like candy as they are that delicious. Nutty, cheesy, this nutritional goodness will melt in your mouth. These oven-roasted cauliflower are on weekly repeat all-year long. The addition of the hemp seeds is such an easy way to boost the protein, fiber, and omega-3s of this classic vegetable.

Servings: *4–6*	**Prep time:** *10 mins*	**Cook time:** *20 mins*

Ingredients

1 head of cauliflower, cut into small florets

1 Tbsp extra virgin olive oil

½ tsp sea salt

1 Tbsp hemp seeds

1 tsp parmesan cheese, freshly grated (optional)

2 garlic cloves minced

Freshly cracked black pepper

Directions

1. Preheat oven to 400 °F (205 °C).
2. Cut cauliflower into bite-sized florets. Rinse under cold water.
3. Transfer to large Ziploc bag.
4. Add olive oil, salt, minced garlic.
5. Shake in bag until evenly coated.
6. On a baking tray lined with parchment paper, pour bag of cauliflower evenly on tray.
7. Sprinkle with hemp seeds and a bit of cracked pepper.
8. Let roast for 20 minutes or until lightly browned and fork-tender (flip halfway through to ensure even cooking).
9. When still hot, toss with parmesan cheese or nutritional yeast.

LE CREUSET

Vegetable Stock

A good stock is a must. I usually prepare large batches of both vegetable and chicken stock, and then freeze to keep on hand. It can be used not only as a basis for soup, but also to add flavor to risotto or sauces. You will need a large stock pot for this recipe, so the vegetables have plenty of space to simmer.

Servings: *n/a*	**Prep time:** *10 mins*	**Cook time:** *2 h+*

Ingredients

1 celery stick, along with leaves

2 carrots, clean but don't peel

1 leek, remove outer tough layers

1 yellow or white onion

1 tsp sea salt

1 bunch of parsley, tied with cooking string

2 cloves of garlic, left whole

13 cups of room temperature water

Optional: vegetable bouillon cube – if you desire a stronger flavor

Directions

1. Prep and clean vegetables.
2. In a large stock pot, add vegetables with water. Add salt.
3. Bring to a boil, then turn to low heat and simmer with lid on for at least 2 hours.
4. When vegetables are soft and broth is lightly flavored, remove all vegetables and strain broth until clear.
5. Let cool before refrigerating.
6. This freezes very well.

Optional chicken stock

1. If you want to make chicken stock, I recommend using a leftover chicken or fresh organic chicken pieces (you can do a mixture of drumsticks and or thighs). Bone in as you want to enjoy all the nourishment found in chicken bones.
2. I would not use carrots when making chicken stock (turns the broth more orange), but I would add sliced carrots if making chicken noodle soup.
3. Simmer chicken and vegetables for at least 2 hours. The chicken should be very soft and falling off the bone.
4. Remove all vegetables and set aside chicken pieces. Strain the broth. Place back on stove. If making chicken soup, scrape the chicken pieces from bones and add back to pot. Add sliced carrots and celery, a bit of dill and bring to a boil. Add your favorite small pasta (elbow macaroni works great).
5. It's an option to add an organic chicken bouillon cube if you desire a stronger flavor.

WEEKDAY DINNER

Let's face it, none of us have time to be preparing elaborate and difficult dinners during the week. Most of us are time-crunched, moving from work to pickups, sports, home work, and bedtime routines. And hopefully a little quiet and rest time to get our bodies and minds prepared to do it all again the next day.

This chapter is filled with recipes that have simple ingredients (if you have a well-stocked pantry and fridge, you can make anything in this chapter with ease), flavors, and the best part is that they can be ready to enjoy within an hour (some even less).

One of my favorite recipes in this chapter is the coconut, lentil, and chick pea dhal with a side of basmati rice. It is a dish that everyone in my family loves (score x5), and usually yields enough leftovers that I can enjoy for lunch the next day (and it may even taste more flavorful).

Of course, these recipes can be interchanged with Sunday dinner, but my goal is to show you that healthy and delicious food can be simply made in a relatively short amount of time.

I can't wait to hear which ones are your favorite weekday dinners.

Italian Orzo Salad

I created this recipe a few years back and it quickly became a family favorite that I usually make for special gatherings. The dressing is so versatile and can be used with any salad. It makes a great side dish or you can even eat it as your main entrée as the combination of beans, arugula, and orzo make it a complete meal.

Servings: *4+*	**Prep time:** *15 mins*	**Cook time:** *n/a*

Ingredients

2 cups cooked orzo

1 can cannellini beans

1 large cucumber, cubed

1 cup baby tomatoes, sliced

¼ cup capers

⅓ cup feta cheese, crumbled

4 cups of arugula, fully packed

Dressing

Juice of 2 lemons

⅓ cup olive oil

2 Tbsp white wine vinegar

½ tsp oregano

Salt and pepper to taste

Directions

1. In a large bowl, combine cooked orzo, navy beans, cucumber, baby tomatoes, capers, and feta cheese.
2. For the dressing combine lemon juice, white wine vinegar, olive oil, cumin, salt and pepper into a mason jar. Shake well until all the ingredients are mixed.
3. Add the arugula and the dressing to the orzo mixture and toss to combine. Adjust the seasoning.
4. Cover and refrigerate the salad for at least 2 hours before serving, this way all the flavors will come together.
5. Enjoy!

Oven-Roasted Chickpeas & Vegetables

Chickpeas and lentils make a hearty, nourishing and satisfying protein addition to your weekly meals. When I first started cooking with legumes and pulses my family didn't love them, but now there are no complaints, especially if the chickpeas are extra soft (or crunchy as in my *Roasted Chickpea* recipe on page 103). This recipe is so delicious served with rice and or whole wheat naan bread to dip in all that creamy curry sauce. Yum!

Servings: *4*	**Prep time:** *10 mins*	**Cook time:** *35 mins*

Ingredients

1⅓ cups dried red lentils

1 Tbsp grapeseed oil

1 yellow onion, diced

1 garlic clove, minced

1 tsp minced ginger

1 Tbsp mild curry powder

½ tsp ground cumin

½ tsp turmeric powder

1 (19 oz) can chickpeas, drained and well rinsed

1 (13.5 fl oz) can coconut milk

2 cups vegetable stock or water

5 oz fresh spinach

Juice of 1 lemon

1 tsp salt (more to taste)

Directions

1. Rinse lentils well under cold running water.
2. Heat oil in a large saucepan over medium-high heat. Add onion, garlic, and ginger sautéing until fragrant, about 1 minute. Stir in curry powder, cumin and turmeric, and cook for another minute.
3. Add rinsed lentils, chickpeas, coconut milk, and vegetable stock to saucepan, stirring to incorporate, before brining mixture to a boil.
4. Reduce heat to a simmer and cook mixture uncovered, stirring occasionally, until lentils are just done, about 30 minutes.
5. Stir in spinach to wilt before adding lemon juice. Season to taste with salt and serve warm over steamed rice or with naan bread.

Tuna Salad Wrap

This is a great wrap, full of bright, fresh flavors. The filling can also be served on baby salad greens or wrapped into collard leaves for a gluten-free alternative.

Servings: *2*	**Prep time:** *15 mins*	**Cook time:** *n/a*

Ingredients

1 cup canned cannellini beans, rinsed and drained

1 garlic clove, minced

2 tsp lemon zest

1 tsp Dijon mustard

2 Tbsp extra virgin olive oil, divided

1 Tbsp fresh parsley, chopped

1 can tuna in water, drained

1 Tbsp fresh basil, chopped

2 Tbsp Kalamata olives, chopped

½ celery rib, finely chopped

½ tomato, diced

1 Tbsp red onion, finely chopped

2 Tbsp red pepper, finely diced

1 tsp lemon juice

2 sprouted whole grain tortilla wraps

½ cup baby arugula leaves, washed and dried

Salt and freshly ground black pepper to taste

Directions

1. In a bowl, coarsely mash beans with a fork. Stir in garlic, lemon zest, mustard, 1 tablespoon olive oil and parsley. Season with a pinch of salt and pepper to taste.
2. In another bowl, break up tuna with a fork or potato masher. Stir in basil, olives, celery, tomato, onion, red pepper, lemon juice, and remaining 1 tablespoon olive oil until well combined. Season to taste with salt and pepper.
3. To assemble wrap, spread bean mixture over tortilla wraps almost to the edge. Evenly divide arugula and tuna mixture down center of wraps. Roll tortilla around filling, cut in half and serve alongside soup or a salad for a filling lunch or dinner.

Black Bean & Lentil Burgers

I have been making a big effort for the past couple of years to make at least one plant-based meal per week. There are many compelling reasons to include more plants in your diet; social and environmental responsibility, budget, health benefits, body weight, and so many more. There is no mistaking that plants are good for us. I have loved experimenting with different legumes as they are such versatile and nutritious forms of protein and healthy fats.

Servings: *4*	**Prep time:** *20 mins*	**Cook time:** *20 mins*

Ingredients

4 tsp coconut oil, divided

½ cup yellow onion, finely chopped

2 Tbsp tahini

½ tsp cumin, ground

½ tsp smoked paprika (optional)

¼ tsp salt

½ tsp black pepper, freshly ground

¾ cups precooked lentils

¾ cups precooked black beans

½ cup carrot, grated

¼ cup fresh cilantro leaves or flat leaf parsley leaves, chopped

4 wholegrain hamburger buns or 8 butter lettuce leaves

Your favorite burger toppings (I love tomato, lettuce, sprouts, and avocado)

Directions

1. In a large frying pan warm 1 teaspoon of oil over medium-high heat. Add onions and sauté until starting to caramelize, about 3 minutes. Remove from heat and allow to cool slightly.
2. Place tahini, cumin, smoked paprika (if using), salt, pepper, lentils, and black beans in a food processor and pulse until beans are coarsely chopped and mixture is well combined. Transfer to a bowl along with sautéed onions, carrots and cilantro, and stir to combine. Divide and shape mixture into four patties.
3. Warm remaining 1 tablespoon oil in a frying pan or cast iron skillet over medium heat. Cook patties, in batches if necessary, until evenly browned and warmed through, about 3–4 minutes on each side. Divide cooked warm patties among hamburger buns or butter lettuce leaves and top with desired toppings.

Tip: These burgers can be easily wrapped into lettuce or served over a bed of greens, and they freeze beautifully when stored in an airtight container between sheets of parchment paper.

Creamy Cauliflower Pasta Sauce

And my family said they didn't like cauliflower. That was until they had it as a creamy sauce poured over their favorite pasta. There are a few variations for the vegetable used in this recipe as Brussels sprouts, peas, asparagus, or mushrooms are all delicious and easy options. If you don't like coconut milk, you could use cream and parmesan cheese, or you could even thin the sauce further to make it a delicious soup. So many possibilities.

Servings: *10*	**Prep time:** *10 mins*	**Cook time:** *25 mins*

Ingredients

1 medium head of cauliflower, cleaned and cut into florets

½ medium leek, sliced

4 cloves of garlic, minced

3 Tbsp olive oil

½ cup nutritional yeast

1 tsp salt

½ tsp black pepper

1 cup vegetable stock

¼ cup full-fat coconut milk (I use canned coconut milk)

Directions

1. Fill a large pot halfway with water and bring to a boil. Add the cauliflower florets to the pot and cook for 15 minutes, or until they are tender.
2. In a small pan sauté the leek in olive oil for 5 minutes, until it's golden brown. Add the garlic and cook for another 2 minutes. Remove from the heat and set aside.
3. Transfer the cauliflower florets into a strainer. Once they cool down, transfer them to a high-speed blender. Add the sautéed garlic and onion, nutritional yeast, salt, pepper, vegetable stock, and coconut milk.
4. Blend on high for 2 minutes, until it becomes creamy.
5. Add this delicious sauce to your favorite pasta dish. You can store the leftover in an airtight container for up to a week in your fridge. Enjoy!

Hemp Seed Basil Pesto

Pesto reminds me of my father-in-law's garden that bursts with fresh basil every August. One of the best ways to savor all the basil throughout the winter months is to turn it into pesto and freeze. Rather than pine nuts, I used hemp seeds which add a nutty flavor and extra nutrition which make this sauce even more satisfying, complete, and delicious by delivering healthy fats and protein.

Servings: *1*	**Prep time:** *10 mins*	**Cook time:** *5 mins*

Ingredients

3 cups tightly packed fresh basil

2 cloves of garlic, chopped

½ cup hemp seeds

¼ cup nutritional yeast or freshly grated parmesan cheese

Juice of 2 medium lemons

¼ cup olive oil

½ tsp salt

Pinch of black pepper

4 Tbsp of water (to thin out the pesto if you like)

Directions

1. Place the basil, garlic, and hemp seeds into a food processor. Pulse for one minute to help break down the basil.
2. Add all the remaining ingredients. Process until smooth, adding one tablespoon of water at a time if you want to thin out the pesto.
3. Adjust the seasoning. At this point I added a pinch of salt for more flavor.
4. Enjoy right away as a dip or use in pasta dishes.
5. Refrigerate the leftover in an airtight container for up to 5 days.

Baked Spinach & Lemon Risotto

Soft, creamy, decadent, and filling, risotto is a classic Italian dish, which traditionally requires a lot of stirring. My baked spinach risotto delivers the rich, creamy flavor, with half the amount of stirring, while letting the oven do the work for you. This is filling enough to be a main course, or it can be a delicious side dish when paired with a white fish such as cod or halibut. This is definitely one of my favorite recipes in the book, and I hope you love it too.

Servings: *6*	**Prep time:** *15 mins*	**Cook time:** *60 mins*

Ingredients

1 Tbsp grapeseed oil or avocado oil

1 cup yellow onions, diced

5 garlic cloves, minced

1 tsp sea salt

½ tsp ground black pepper

2 cups brown Arborio rice

2 Tbsp lemon zest, finely grated

1 Tbsp thyme leaves, freshly chopped or 1 tsp dried thyme

1 tsp red pepper flakes (optional)

10 oz chopped frozen spinach, thawed and excess water squeezed out

4 cups unsalted chicken broth

1¼ cups hot water

1 cup finely grated Parmesan cheese, plus extra for serving

Directions

1. Preheat oven to 375 °F (190 °C).
2. Heat oil in a 5.5 L or 6 L Dutch oven over medium heat. Add onions and cook, stirring frequently, until translucent and starting to brown, about 4 minutes.
3. Stir in garlic, salt, and pepper, and continue to cook another 2 minutes. Stir in rice and cook until toasted and just beginning to brown, about 3 minutes.
4. Add lemon zest, thyme leaves, red pepper flakes (if using), and spinach to the mixture. Stir until spinach has warmed through, about 2 minutes.
5. Pour chicken broth and water over rice mixture and bring liquid to a simmer. Stir in cheese before placing Dutch oven in preheated oven and cook uncovered for 20 minutes.
6. Stir rice mixture and continue to bake until liquid is absorbed and mixture is creamy, another 20–25 minutes. If rice mixture is still slightly crunchy, add more hot water or chicken broth about ⅓ cup at a time and bake another 10–15 minutes.
7. Once baked, allow risotto to cool for 10–15 minutes. Serve with an additional sprinkling of parmesan cheese if desired.

Tip: Any leftovers will keep refrigerated in an airtight container for up to 3 days. If risotto mixture becomes too thick during storage, loosen while heating with additional water or broth.

Green Coconut Curry

I love a good curry, especially one that gives you a hearty blend of vegetables and protein all in one. Served on delicious golden rice this will definitely become one of your favorite go-to weekday recipes.

Servings: *4*	**Prep time:** *15 mins*	**Cook time:** *45 mins*

Ingredients

Green coconut curry

- 1 small yellow onion, chopped
- 2 garlic cloves, minced
- 8 oz frozen spinach, slightly thawed
- 2 Tbsp green curry paste
- 1 Tbsp coconut sugar
- ¼ tsp sea salt
- 1 (14 oz) can coconut milk
- 1 cup vegetable broth or water
- 1 medium sweet potato, cut into ½-inch cubes (about 1 cup total)
- ½ cup carrot, chopped
- ½ cup broccoli florets
- ½ cup red bell pepper, chopped
- ½ cup cherry tomatoes, cut in half
- ⅓ cup snow peas, cut into thirds

Golden coconut rice

- 1 cup Jasmine brown rice
- 1¼ cups coconut milk
- 1 cup water
- ¼ tsp ground turmeric powder
- ¼ tsp salt
- 2 Tbsp unsweetened shredded coconut

Directions

1. Start by making golden coconut rice. In a medium saucepan stir together rice, coconut milk, water, turmeric, salt, and shredded coconut. Place over medium-high heat and bring to a boil. Reduce heat to low, cover saucepan and simmer until all liquid has evaporated, about 35–40 minutes. Remove saucepan from heat and keeping covered, set aside for 10 minutes. Fluff rice with a fork and serve.
2. While rice is simmering, make curry. In a large saucepan, heat oil over medium heat. Add onion and garlic, and cook, stirring frequently, until just starting to brown. Stir in spinach, green curry paste, coconut sugar, and salt; cook until spinach is soft, about 3 minutes.
3. Add coconut milk and broth and bring to a simmer. Remove saucepan from heat and, using an immersion blender (or transfer to a high-power blender), blend spinach mixture until smooth. Taste and adjust seasoning with more curry paste, coconut sugar, or salt.
4. Return saucepan to medium heat and bring to a simmer. Add sweet potatoes and carrots; cook until softened, about 10 minutes. Add broccoli and red pepper; continue to cook for another 3 minutes. Finally, stir in tomatoes and snow peas allowing to cook, stirring occasionally, for an additional 4–5 minutes. Broccoli, peppers, and snow peas should all be crisp tender. Taste and adjust seasoning as desired. Serve warm over golden coconut rice.

Tip: Use whatever vegetables you have on hand in this curry. Also feel free to add cubed chicken breast, chunks of salmon, or tofu for added protein and kid appeal.

Spicy Turmeric Cauliflower Tacos

If you're looking to give your taco Tuesday a yummy twist, you will love these spicy turmeric roasted cauliflower tacos. If your family doesn't love a lot of spice you can leave the buffalo sauce off. There are so many options for preparing the cauliflower. I have also taken the *Roasted Cauliflower with Hemp Seeds* recipe on page 193 and rolled these into a tortilla topped with guacamole and all the fixings.

Servings: *6+*	**Prep time:** *20 mins**	**Cook time:** *30 mins*

Ingredients

Spicy cauliflower

- 1 head of medium cauliflower cut into florets
- 2 cups oat flour
- 1 Tbsp garlic powder
- 1 tsp salt
- ½ tsp black pepper
- ½ tsp turmeric
- 1 cup buffalo hot sauce

Cashew sauce

- 1 cup cashews soaked for 1 h
- 2 garlic cloves
- 3 Tbsp nutritional yeast
- Juice of one medium lemon
- ½ tsp salt
- ¼ cup water
- ¾ cup full-fat coconut milk

Fillings & base

- 6 corn/whole wheat tortillas
- Sautéed mushrooms
- Avocado (or guacamole)
- Peas
- Corn
- Cilantro
- Jalapeños
- Freshly squeezed lime juice

Directions

1. Preheat oven to 450 °F (230 °C). Line a baking sheet with parchment paper and set aside.
2. Prepare the batter for the cauliflower by combining the almond milk, oat flour, and seasonings in a medium bowl (except the buffalo sauce). Mix until batter is combined.
3. Dip the cauliflower in the batter, shaking off excess batter before placing the cauliflower on a baking sheet.
4. Bake for 25–30 minutes until golden brown.
5. While the cauliflower is baking combine all the sauce ingredients in a blender and blend until smooth. Set aside.
6. When the cauliflower is ready, remove it from the baking sheet and toss it in the buffalo hot sauce mixture (this part is optional, if you don't like spice, skip this step).
7. Heat each corn tortilla in a skillet and fill with the buffalo cauliflower, your choice of fillings and cashew sauce.

*+1 h for cashews to soak

Peanut Butter Pasta

Peanut butter + pasta, need I say more. If you have never enjoyed a smooth, creamy peanut butter sauce, now's your chance, and trust me, this easy, flavorful dish will quickly become a favorite, and not just for your kids.

Servings: *4*	**Prep time:** *10 mins*	**Cook time:** *10 mins*

Ingredients

¼ cup smooth peanut butter, unsalted

3 Tbsp reduced sodium soy sauce or tamari

3 garlic cloves, minced

2 Tbsp honey

1 Tbsp ginger, finely grated

1 Tbsp rice vinegar

1 tsp sesame oil

1 tsp Sriracha hot sauce (optional)

7–8 oz noodles of your choice

1 Tbsp avocado oil

2 Tbsp water

2 cups broccoli florets

2 green onions, trimmed and thinly sliced

2 carrots, peeled and shredded

1 red bell pepper, cut into strips

1 cup snow peas, trimmed

2 tsp sesame seeds, toasted

Directions

1. In a medium bowl, whisk together peanut butter, soy sauce, garlic, honey, ginger, vinegar, sesame oil, and hot sauce, if using. Set aside.
2. Cook pasta of choice according to package directions. Drain well and set aside.
3. Heat avocado oil and water together in a large skillet over medium heat. Once simmering add broccoli florets and cover, cooking broccoli until crisp tender, about 2–3 minutes.
4. Remove cover and let excess water evaporate for a minute. Stir in green onions, grated carrot, pepper, and snow peas. Cook, stirring often, until warmed through, about 1–2 minutes.
5. Add cooked noodles and peanut butter mixture, tossing until well combined and pasta is warm, about 2 minutes. Serve immediately garnished with toasted sesame seeds, if desired.

Tip: You can substitute the peanut butter for almond butter with equally delicious results.

Lemony Veggie Frittata

Eggs for dinner – yes please. Many of us think about omelets or frittatas for weekend brunch or as a breakfast food, but they actually make the perfect meal for those evenings when you want something quick, fresh, and ready in one dish. Serve with crusty bread.

Servings: *5–6*	**Prep time:** *20 mins*	**Cook time:** *20 mins*

Ingredients

2 Tbsp olive oil

½ cup onion, sliced

1 cup mushroom, sliced

½ cup red pepper, julienned

3 medium zucchini, julienned

2 garlic cloves, minced

6 large eggs

½ cup parmesan cheese, grated

¼ cup chives, chopped

2 Tbsp fresh lemon juice

2 Tbsp fresh parsley, chopped

½ Tbsp basil, chopped

1 sprig dill

½ tsp salt

¼ tsp pepper

1 cup shredded mozzarella cheese

Directions

1. In a medium-sized skillet, sauté the onion and mushrooms in olive oil for 5 minutes.
2. Add the pepper, zucchini, and garlic; sauté for another 5 minutes.
3. In a separate mixing bowl, whip the eggs, lemon juice, grated parmesan, chives, parsley, dill, salt, and pepper.
4. Pour evenly over skillet and sprinkle with the mozzarella cheese. Cover and cook over low heat for 15 minutes.
5. Loosen the edges with a spatula and invert onto a serving plate.

Fish Taco

I love fish tacos, and they are always something I order in restaurants, with extra guacamole of course. I also find these fish tacos to be easy weeknight dinners especially when we are eating in shifts. The fish keeps well once baked, and the tortillas can be warmed as needed.

Servings: *4–8*	**Prep time:** *20 mins*	**Cook time:** *20 mins*

Ingredients

Fish

- 1 lb halibut or cod fish
- ¼ cup avocado oil
- 1 tsp dried oregano
- 1 tsp smoked Spanish paprika
- ¼ tsp red pepper flakes (optional)
- ¼ tsp garlic powder
- 1 lemon juiced
- ½ tsp salt
- ¼ tsp freshly ground black pepper

Lime coleslaw

- 3 Tbsp lime juice
- 3 Tbsp rice vinegar
- 2 garlic cloves
- ½ tsp salt
- ½ cup grapeseed oil
- ½ cup fresh cilantro leaves
- 1½ cups shredded purple cabbage
- 1 carrot, grated
- ½ red bell pepper, thinly sliced

To assemble tacos

- 8 small corn tortillas
- Guacamole (optional)
- Hot sauce (optional)

Directions

1. Preheat oven to 400 °F (205 °C).
2. Rinse fish under cold water and pat dry with a paper towel. Cut into 2-inch pieces.
3. In a bowl, whisk together oil, lemon juice, and herbs. Add fish and gently stir to coat in marinade. Refrigerate for at least 30 minutes or if you're short on time, cook immediately.
4. Lightly spray the bottom of an oven-safe baking dish. Lay fish in dish. Bake for 20 minutes or until fish is flaky.
5. Meanwhile, in a blender, combine lime juice, vinegar, garlic, salt, and grapeseed oil on high speed until creamy. Add cilantro and blend until dressing is flecked with green.
6. Place cabbage, carrot, and bell pepper in a large bowl. Drizzle with dressing to taste and toss until vegetables are well coated. Set aside.
7. To assemble, warm tortillas on both sides in a clean frying pan over medium heat. Top warm tortilla with lime coleslaw and a few pieces of fish. Garnish with a dollop of guacamole, and serve with your favorite hot sauce, if desired.

Butternut Squash Noodles with Pesto Chicken

Sweet, garlicky, and a completely satisfying weeknight "pasta" dinner – trust me, you won't miss the regular pasta. You could always serve this pesto and chicken with your favorite pasta. Remember it's your kitchen and there are no rules. Let your creativity and senses guide the choices you make for your family dinner.

Servings: *4*	**Prep time:** *20 mins*	**Cook time:** *15 mins*

Ingredients

¼ cup sunflower seeds

1 garlic clove

1 Tbsp lemon juice

2 Tbsp Parmesan cheese, shredded (or nutritional yeast)

½ tsp salt

2 Tbsp extra virgin olive oil

2 cups packed spinach leaves

1 cup packed basil leaves

2 chicken breasts, cut into 1-inch pieces

1 medium butternut squash, peeled and seeded

1 Tbsp grapeseed oil

24 cherry tomatoes

Directions

1. To make pesto sauce in a food processor or blender, pulse sunflower seeds, garlic, lemon juice, Parmesan, and salt until coarsely chopped. Add olive oil, spinach and basil, and blend until sauce is well combined. Sauce may be made very smooth or left a little chunky. Set aside.
2. In a small bowl, toss together 2 tablespoons of pesto sauce with chicken and set aside to marinade for 2 minutes.
3. Meanwhile, make butternut squash noodles. Using a spiralizer cut squash into long, thin noodles resembling spaghetti. Set aside.
4. Heat oil in a wok or large skillet over medium-high heat. Add cherry tomatoes and sauté until they have colored and started to burst, about another 3 minutes. Transfer to a small bowl and set aside.
5. Place wok back over medium-high heat and add chicken. Sauté until just cooked through, about 4–5 minutes. Add butternut squash noodles and, tossing occasionally, cook until slightly softened, about 4 minutes.
6. Add a couple of heaping tablespoons of pesto sauce and toss until noodles are covered in sauce. Fold in tomatoes and heat until warmed through, about 1 minute. Serve while warm with additional pesto sauce, if desired.

One-Pan Lemon Chicken Bake

Sheet dinners make weeknight cooking a breeze and honestly this dish could also be prepared with fish such as salmon or cod. I also love the convenience of being able to cook and serve from the same dish which also makes clean up so much easier. The flavors come together so nicely with the rosemary and lemon. If you prefer extra sauce, increase the amount of lemon used.

Servings: *4–5*	**Prep time:** *10 mins*	**Cook time:** *50 mins*

Ingredients

1½ lb baby new potatoes

1 bunch asparagus, woody ends trimmed and discarded (or green beans work well)

1 red bell pepper, chopped into 1-inch chunks

1 yellow bell pepper, chopped into 1-inch chunks

1 garlic bulb, cloves separated

1 Tbsp grapeseed oil or avocado oil

Salt and ground black pepper, to taste

1 lemon, cut in half

2 tsp rosemary sprigs, chopped

8 skin on chicken drumsticks

Directions

1 Preheat oven to 350 °F (175 °C).

2 Toss together potatoes, peppers, garlic, and oil in a large roasting pan baking dish. Season with a good pinch each of salt and ground pepper. Squeeze juice from lemon halves over vegetables before cutting lemon into chunks and adding to roasting pan. Toss everything together once more before covering roasting pan with aluminum foil and placing in hot oven for 15 minutes. While vegetables are cooking, season chicken with salt and pepper.

3 After 15 minutes, remove foil and mix rosemary into vegetables. Arrange chicken drumsticks on top of vegetables. Return to oven and continue to cook until potatoes are tender and chicken is cooked through, about 40 minutes. Add the asparagus for the last 8 minutes. Serve lemony chicken in pan allowing everyone to help themselves.

4 Garnish with a sprinkle of parmesan cheese if desired.

Sweet & Spicy Turkey Chili

As a kid, I hated chili… it was one of those dinners that I reluctantly ate while plugging my nose. I know for sure, I dislike kidney beans (one of the only beans I don't like), and I didn't love spicy food (now I love it). As a busy, health-conscious mom, one pot, and slow-cooker dinners are a weekday savior. So one of my goals was to find the right combination of beans, spice, and everything nice that my family could enjoy on a cold-winter night.

Servings: *6–8*	**Prep time:** *20 mins*	**Cook time:** *45 mins*

Ingredients

2 tsp extra virgin olive oil

1 medium yellow onion, chopped

3 garlic cloves, minced

1 medium red bell pepper, chopped

1 pound extra lean ground turkey

2 Tbsp chili powder

2 tsp ground cumin

1 tsp dried oregano

Pinch cayenne pepper

½ tsp salt, plus more to taste

1 (28 oz) can diced tomatoes or crushed tomatoes

1¼ cups chicken broth

1 can organic black beans (drained and rinsed)

1 can organic cannellini beans (drained and rinsed)

1 cup organic sweet corn kernels (if using frozen, thaw before adding)

Toppings

Grated cheese, avocado, jalapeño, tortilla chips, cilantro, sour cream, or Greek yogurt.

Directions

1. Place oil in a large pot over medium-high heat. Add in onion, garlic, and red pepper and sauté for 5–7 minutes, stirring frequently. Next add in ground turkey and break up the meat; cooking until no longer pink. Next add in chili powder, cumin, oregano, cayenne pepper, and salt; stir for about 20 seconds.
2. Next add in tomatoes, chicken broth, beans, and corn. Bring to a boil, then reduce heat and simmer for 30–45 minutes or until chili thickens and flavors come together. Taste and adjust seasonings and salt as necessary.

Tip: The first thing I did was use ground turkey – I enjoy this much more than beef. And instead of kidney beans, I use black and cannellini beans. The sweetness comes from the corn, which in my opinion is a must in chili. And voila, the healthiest and most delicious chili around. I hope this chili makes you feel cozy and nourished.

This recipe was inspired by Monique of the Ambitious Kitchen.

Crispy Panko Hemp Halibut

This recipe is inspired from my love of *Pajo's Fish & Chips* at the Rocky Point Marina in Port Moody. This is such a special treat for our family, and it just feels good. However, rather than deep frying, I bake these and add lots of hemp seeds for the crust to make them extra rich in protein, fiber, and healthy fats. The trick to getting them crispy – brush the top layer with avocado oil. This allows the crust to bake crispy golden.

Servings: *4*	**Prep time:** *20 mins*	**Cook time:** *20 mins*

Ingredients

Crispy halibut

- ¼ cup whole wheat pastry flour (or oat flour also works)
- 1 tsp salt
- ¼ tsp freshly ground black pepper
- 1 large egg
- 1½ cups whole wheat panko breadcrumbs
- ¼ cup hemp hearts
- 3 Tbsp fresh parsley, chopped
- ¼ cup grated parmesan cheese (or nutritional yeast)
- 1½ lb halibut fillets, skinned, boned, and cut into 1-inch wide pieces
- 2 Tbsp avocado oil

Optional yogurt tartar sauce

- ¾ cup Greek yogurt
- ¼ cup dill pickle, chopped
- 1 Tbsp capers, chopped
- 2 Tbsp red onion, finely chopped
- 1 Tbsp lemon juice
- 1 Tbsp fresh parsley, chopped
- 1 Tbsp fresh dill, chopped
- 1 tsp Dijon mustard

Directions

1. Preheat oven to 450 °F (230 °C).
2. Whisk together flour, salt, and pepper.
3. In another bowl, whisk egg.
4. In a third bowl, stir together panko, hemp, parsley, and parmesan.
5. Brush a parchment lined baking tray with some of the avocado oil.
6. Working with one piece of halibut at a time, dip into flour and shake off any excess. Dip into egg mixture and let excess drip off. Pat into panko mixture so that an even coating adheres to all sides of the fish.
7. Place coated fish on prepared baking tray and repeat with remaining halibut pieces. Once all pieces have been coated, using a pastry brush, lightly brush each piece all over with avocado oil (or you can use the spray style avocado oil which is super easy).
8. Meanwhile stir together all sauce ingredients in a bowl and refrigerate until ready to use.
9. Bake halibut until crust is golden brown and fish is cooked through and flakes easily, about 18–20 minutes.
10. To serve, divide halibut among serving plates and place a dollop of sauce along side. To round out the meal, serve alongside steamed broccoli, if desired.

Cedar Plank Salmon with Maple-Dijon Glaze

Fire up your grill and enjoy the beauty of spring time with this cedar plank maple salmon that is sure to win over your entire family, even those that think they don't like fish. This is my kids' favorite way to eat salmon. The sweetness of the maple and the aroma and taste from the plank gives the most delicious flavor. This dish is quick and easy to prepare and makes a great weeknight dinner.

Servings: *4*	**Prep time:** *5 mins + 30 mins**	**Cook time:** *15 mins*

Ingredients

Large cedar plank (can be purchased in most grocery stores near the fish section, or at your local fish monger)

1–1½ lb of salmon (in filet form with skin on) – I like spring, or sockeye

¼ cup maple syrup

2 Tbsp grainy Dijon mustard

½ tsp salt

¼ tsp black pepper

Directions

1. Soak a cedar plank in water for at least 40 minutes (the longer the better) – this is to prevent flames on the grill.
2. Wash salmon filet and pat dry with paper towel. Sprinkle salt and pepper over the salmon.
3. In a small bowl, whisk the maple syrup and mustard. Brush half of the salmon with the glaze in a baking dish for about 30 minutes.
4. Place plank on grill over medium heat. Lay salmon filet on top. Brush remaining maple mixture. Close lid and let cook for about 20 minutes or until fish easily flakes. (Check it regularly to avoid fire spots, and overcooking the fish).

*For marinating

STAUB

Roasted Salmon with Spinach Chimichurri

Growing up in the prairies, eating a lot of fish (outside of lake fish), was not really an option. Ever since moving to the beautiful West Coast, I continually marvel at my local fish mongers' selection of pristine, wild fish, especially salmon. We devote one night a week to salmon, and it's one of the most flavorful and easy to prepare of all the fish. The drizzle of chimichurri makes this dish so moist and delicious.

Servings: *4*	**Prep time:** *10 mins*	**Cook time:** *15 mins*

Ingredients

1 cup packed baby spinach leaves

1 or 2 garlic cloves, peeled and smashed

2 Tbsp packed fresh oregano or 1½ tsp dried oregano

2 Tbsp red wine vinegar

¼ tsp hot red pepper flakes

¼ tsp salt

Pinch ground black pepper

½ cup extra virgin olive oil

2 zucchini, cut into 1-inch pieces

20 cherry tomatoes, cut in half

1 tsp salt, divided

1½ Tbsp avocado oil

2 tsp lemon juice

¼ tsp ground black pepper

4 skinless salmon fillets, about 5 oz each

Directions

1. Preheat oven to 425 °F (220 °C).
2. To make spinach chimichurri place spinach, garlic, oregano, vinegar, pepper flakes, salt, and pepper in a food processor or blender. Pulse together until mixture is finely chopped; stopping and scraping down the sides of bowl with a rubber spatula as needed. With motor running, add oil in a steady stream. Scrape down the sides of bowl again and pulse until mixture is well combined. Sauce should still have some texture to it. Transfer to a bowl and set aside while roasting salmon. Spinach chimichurri will keep refrigerated in an airtight container for up to one week.
3. Place zucchini and tomatoes on a baking dish large enough to hold them in a single layer. Sprinkle with ½ tsp salt.
4. In a small bowl, whisk together oil, lemon juice, black pepper, and remaining ½ tsp salt.
5. Place fish on zucchini and tomatoes before drizzling oil mixture on top. Let sit 10 minutes. Roast until fish is just firm and flakes easily, about 8–12 minutes depending on the thickness of your fillets.
6. Serve roasted zucchini and tomatoes topped with a piece of roasted salmon and a drizzle of spinach chimichurri sauce.

Tip: Cooking and serving it in the same dish makes clean up a breeze. Save your chimichurri sauce to use on top of other fish, chicken, beef, or legumes.

Weeknight Skillet Paella

Your family won't believe you prepared and served this all in the same pot. There are honestly no rules with paellas and you could easily sub in so many different vegetables or protein choices. Serve alongside a green tossed salad for a nourishing weeknight dinner.

Servings: *4*	**Prep time:** *15 mins*	**Cook time:** *15 mins*

Ingredients

3 skinless, boneless chicken thighs, cut into ½-inch pieces

½ tsp salt

¼ tsp ground black pepper

½ tsp smoked paprika

1 Tbsp grapeseed oil

1 small yellow onion

3 garlic cloves, minced

1½ cups Arborio rice

3 cups unsalted chicken broth

1 (14 oz) can diced tomatoes

1 cup frozen peas

12 oz large raw shrimp, peeled and deveined

½ lemon

1 Tbsp flat leaf parsley leaves, chopped (optional)

Directions

1. In a small bowl, stir together chicken, salt, pepper, and smoked paprika until chicken is well coated in seasoning.
2. Heat oil in a large 9- or 10-inch skillet over medium heat. Add seasoned chicken and cook, stirring occasionally, until browned, about 3 minutes. Transfer to a plate and set aside.
3. Add onion to skillet and cook, stirring often, until translucent, about 4 minutes. Stir in garlic and let cook until fragrant, about 30 seconds. Stir in rice and, stirring occasionally, cook until lightly toasted, 3–4 minutes. Stir broth and diced tomatoes along with their juices into rice mixture.
4. Cover and cook without stirring for 12 minutes. Stir in chicken, cover, and continue to cook without stirring until most of the liquid has absorbed into rice, about another 5–8 minutes.
5. Scatter peas and shrimp over rice, cover again and cook until shrimp is pink and opaque, 3–4 minutes. Remove skillet from heat, squeeze juice from half a lemon over skillet paella before sprinkling with chopped parsley, if desired. Serve immediately.

SUNDAY DINNER

When I was growing up, Sunday was an extraordinary day of the week. We went to mass every Sunday morning, and in our house going to church was non-negotiable. Every store in our small farming community was closed. My dad, napped in his chair after a long week of farming, while my mom cooked a fresh, delicious, farm style "supper". I remember being bored as a child on these long Sundays, without much to do, other than rest, read, or try to get my younger siblings to play with me. Times were different, social media and video games didn't exist, shopping online was unheard of, and well, Sunday was intended to be a day of rest and reflection.

Now I'm a mother with my own family. I try to keep activities and sports to a minimum on Sunday to have enough time to build and nurture these precious moments. We still attend and are actively involved in our church community. I'm very proud of our family values that have come together by design.

I also cherish setting aside this one day a week to enjoy a more elaborate meal together as a family (it's a great opportunity to braise or roast your favorite cut of meat, or prepare lasagna, and maybe even dessert), opening a bottle of wine for the grown-ups and spending time sharing stories of our week. These meals are getting "easier" and more enjoyable now that the kids are growing up a bit. I actually get to sit down at the table, rather than continually feeding, cleaning, or both. Spending time without cell phones or video games is a gift because in these moments we genuinely connect and we are all allowed into the hearts and minds of one another. Our heart-to-heart talks around our table make our house a home, and these memories will live on in all of us forever.

The time you dedicate to your family each week is valuable because their health and happiness depend on more than just the food you eat. Nurturing, connecting with each other and spending time creating family memories over a delicious meal is crucial not only for your happiness index, but ultimately for your families' total health and well-being!

Now, obviously this particular day or time shared doesn't have to be on Sunday, it can be any day of the week that fits your busy schedule. I hope to encourage you to safeguard one precious day or evening each week that is for you and your loved ones. These moments can also be shared with extended family, or friends that are like family building memories that you can look back on and share with each other time and time again.

What I know for sure is many years from now you will look back, and remember fondly, all the memories of your version of that special Sunday dinner.

Braised Cauliflower & Kale

I don't watch a lot of TV, but on Sunday afternoons if we're home, my favorite show to turn on is *Lidia's Kitchen*. She is my favorite Italian chef to watch as I find her advice so practical. Her recipes are so delicious and because it's Italian food, anything I cook from her show or cookbooks is loved by my entire family. This braised cauliflower is outstanding! I have modified the recipe slightly from her original version to bring even more nutrition to this delightful dish.

Servings: *4*	**Prep time:** *10 mins*	**Cook time:** *30 mins*

Ingredients

2 Tbsp extra virgin olive oil

4 oz coconut bacon (or pancetta)

1 large onion, sliced

1 large head of cauliflower, cored but tender leaves left on

1 (28 oz) can plum tomatoes crushed by hand

1 tsp sea salt

¼ tsp red pepper flakes

1 bunch of dinosaur kale leaves torn from stem

Directions

1. In a large Dutch oven pot, add extra virgin olive oil and coconut bacon. Cook until browned.
2. Add sliced onions and let cook until translucent.
3. Place whole cauliflower bottom side down in pot.
4. Pour in tomatoes alongside 1 cup of water sloshed from the can of tomatoes to clean it out.
5. Season with sea salt and red pepper flakes.
6. Bring to a simmer and cover. Let cook for 25 minutes or until fork-tender, but not falling apart.
7. The last 5 minutes, add the chopped kale around the cauliflower and let wilt.
8. Remove cauliflower and transfer to a cutting board. Slice into wedges and serve with kale and extra sauce.

Tip: Serve by itself as a side dish, on spiralized butternut squash or zucchini, or on top a bed of pasta. Just when you thought you may have given up on cauliflower, along comes this beauty of a recipe. *Delicioso!*

Roasted Vegetable Lasagna

Lasagna is my favorite Italian dish of all time. It is a pure labor of love as there are many moving parts and it takes some time to put it all together. This is a great dish to serve for guests or a family Sunday dinner, and then enjoy the leftovers the next day. Lasagna actually tastes better the next day as all the flavors had a chance to blend together and intensify.

Servings: *10–12*	**Prep time:** *45 mins**	**Cook time:** *35 mins + time for it to rest*

Ingredients

Roasted vegetables

- 1 large leek, halved, white and light green parts coarsely chopped and rinsed well
- 2 carrots, sliced into thin rounds
- 1 cup cremini mushrooms, stem trimmed, sliced in half
- 1 zucchini sliced into ¼-inch moons
- 12 cherry tomatoes
- 1 red bell pepper, sliced
- Extra virgin olive oil for drizzling
- Sea salt and freshly ground black pepper

Cashew béchamel sauce

- 2 Tbsp olive oil
- 1 small sweet onion, diced
- 1½ cup of cashews, soaked for 3 h
- 1 garlic clove, diced
- Juice of 1 medium lemon
- 1 cup of water
- ¼ cup vegetable stock
- ½ tsp sea salt

Traditional béchamel sauce

- 6 Tbsp butter
- 3½ Tbsp flour
- 2 cups warmed milk

Directions

1. Heat the olive oil on medium. Cook the onion for about 2–3 minutes until soft. You want to avoid getting any color on them.
2. Transfer the onions into a blender or a food processor along with the remaining ingredients (cashews, garlic, lemon juice, water, chicken stock, and salt).
3. Blend until very smooth and creamy. Adjust the consistency by adding more water, one tablespoon at a time to reach that pouring cream consistency.
4. Serve with your favorite dish.

Directions *(traditional béchamel sauce)*

5. Melt butter on stove. Add flour and stir with wooden spoon. It will be thick. Let it cook on medium heat for about 3 minutes stirring constantly. Slowly start adding warmed milk, whisking constantly so it doesn't burn.
6. Gradually add the rest of the milk whisking until a thick sauce forms.
7. Add ¼ tsp salt once thick.

*Plus time for cashews to soak

Roasted Vegetable Lasagna *cont.*

There are so many styles and options when creating lasagna. You can make a traditional lasagna using meat and tomato sauce, or you can make a vegetable or a combination of both. There are really no rules when creating this dish, so I've provided a few different options for the sauces and layers. Feel free to mix and match, and use the vegetables that you like.

Servings: *10–12*	**Prep time:** *45 mins*	**Cook time:** *35 mins + time for it to rest*

Ingredients

Ricotta filling

- 17 oz ricotta cheese
- 1 egg
- ¼ cup parmesan cheese, grated
- 8 oz frozen spinach, thawed and excess water removed
- Juice and zest of 1 lemon
- ¼ tsp red pepper flakes
- 1 tsp sea salt
- Fresh black pepper

Lasagna assembly

- 12 lasagna noodles (you can use regular, whole wheat, or spinach is also delicious)
- 1 jar of your favorite pasta sauce (or you can make your pasta sauce yourself – see recipe on page 207)
- 1 cup packed kale, chopped
- 1 log of fresh mozzarella cheese, sliced in thin slices to cover the top (or you can use shredded mozzarella)
- Sliced basil for garnish

Directions

1. Preheat oven to 425 °F (220 °C).
2. Line a large baking sheet with parchment paper. Place vegetables on the sheet and toss with drizzle of olive oil and pinches of salt and pepper. Roast for 20–25 minutes or until golden brown. Remove vegetables from oven and reduce heat to 375 °F (190 °C).
3. Make the ricotta filling by mixing all ingredients in a large bowl. Set aside.
4. Make your choice of béchamel sauce.
5. In a large pot of generously salted water, prepare the noodles.
6. Assemble the lasagna. Drizzle bottom of 9 x 13-inch baking pan with olive oil. Spread 1 cup of marina sauce into bottom of baking dish and cover with 3–4 lasagna noodles. Spread the ricotta mixture, half the roasted vegetables, half the béchamel, half chopped kale, and ⅔ cup sauce. Add next layer of noodles and top with the remaining ingredients. Top last layer of noodles with remaining sauce, béchamel, mozzarella cheese, and fresh basil for garnish. Drizzle with olive oil.
7. Bake at 375 °F (190 °C) for 25–30 minutes or until brown and bubbly. Cover loosely with foil if it's becoming too brown. Let sit for 20 minutes to settle before slicing. Garnish with parmesan cheese and fresh basil leaves.

Tip: If you're making your own tomato sauce, this is also something you could prepare the day before in order to speed-up preparation on the day you are serving.

Cashew Cream Sauce

If you're looking for an alternative to cream sauce for pastas or vegetables, this cashew cream sauce is so delicious. I have used it in everything from Brussels sprouts, lasagna, or any other pasta. Dairy free, gluten free, and vegan (when using vegetable stock rather than chicken stock), this is the ultimate "cream" sauce.

Servings: *2*	**Prep time:** *10 mins**	**Cook time:** *20 mins*

Ingredients

2 Tbsp olive oil

1 small sweet onion, diced

1½ cup of cashews, soaked for 3 hours

1 garlic clove, diced

Juice of 1 medium lemon

1 cup of water

¼ cup chicken stock

½ tsp sea salt

Directions

1 Heat the olive oil on medium. Cook the onion for about 2–3 minutes until it softens. You want to avoid getting any color on them.

2 Transfer the onions into a blender or a food processor along with the remaining ingredients (cashews, garlic, lemon juice, water, chicken stock, and salt).

3 Blend until very smooth and creamy. Adjust the consistency by adding more water, one tablespoon at a time to reach that pouring cream consistency.

4 Serve with your favorite dish.

* Plus time for cashews to soak.

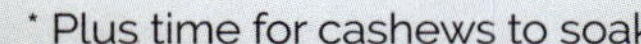

Sunflower Seed Alfredo Sauce

Creamy, delicious, thick, you will have a hard time believing this "alfredo" sauce has no cream in it. Nuts and seeds are rich in healthy fats, therefore when soaked and blended make the base for a delicious and nutritious sauce. This sauce can be used as a veggie dip (hot or cold), poured over your favorite pasta or spiralized vegetable dish or as a cream layer in lasagna.

Servings: *6*	**Prep time:** *10 mins (plus soaking time)*	**Cook time:** *5 mins*

Ingredients

1 cup raw sunflower seeds, soaked for 6 hours or overnight

½ cup filtered water

2 garlic cloves, peeled

¼ cup yellow onion, diced

2 Tbsp nutritional yeast

4 Tbsp fresh lemon juice

½ tsp white wine vinegar

1 tsp salt

½ tsp paprika

Black pepper to taste

Directions

1. Add the sunflower seeds and all the remaining ingredients to a high-speed blender.
2. Blend for 2 minutes on high, or until smooth.
3. Adjust the consistency by adding more water.
4. Use right away or store in an airtight container in the fridge for up to a week.

Tip: You can make the sauce without using any onions as well.

Pumpkin Marinara Sauce

This delicious pumpkin marinara sauce will be on repeat during the fall season when our taste palate craves pumpkin, squash, and cozy warm flavors. I cheated a little by using canned pumpkin rather than making it from scratch, but this allows this sauce to be used on a busy weeknight dinner.

Servings: *4*	**Prep time:** *10 mins*	**Cook time:** *20 mins*

Ingredients

1 Tbsp grapeseed oil

1 yellow onion, chopped

1 red bell pepper, seeded and chopped

2 garlic cloves, minced

½ tsp oregano, dried

1 tsp basil, dried

¼ tsp cinnamon, ground

1 (14.5 oz) can diced tomatoes

1 (14 oz) can organic pumpkin puree

1 tsp balsamic vinegar

1 tsp salt

Ground black pepper, to taste

Directions

1. Warm oil in a medium saucepan over medium heat. Add onions and peppers and cook, stirring often, until very tender, about 10 minutes. Stir in garlic, oregano, basil, and cinnamon; cook until fragrant, about 1 minute.
2. Add tomatoes along with their juices and cook stirring for 1 minute.
3. Stir in pumpkin, bring to a simmer and let cook, stirring often, for 5 minutes.
4. Transfer warm tomato mixture to a blender before adding balsamic vinegar, salt, and a good pinch of pepper. Puree until smooth and creamy. Season to taste with additional salt, pepper, and vinegar as desired.

Tip: Swirled into your favorite pasta, drizzled over roasted vegetables, or even grilled chicken or white fish such as cod or halibut, you will find so many versatile ways to incorporate this one into your week.

Cashew Butternut Squash Alfredo Sauce

Nuts and seeds make the most delicious and creamy base for sauces without any cream at all. You won't believe it yourself (and I know as I've had several people test these recipes and couldn't believe there wasn't any cream used). The addition of the butternut squash gives a beautiful color, and slightly sweet flavor. It is one of my favorite fall vegetables, and I love using it as a nourishing addition to this dip.

Servings: *4*	**Prep time:** *5 mins*	**Cook time:** *20 mins*

Ingredients

¾ cup raw cashews

2 cup vegetable broth, divided

1 Tbsp grapeseed oil or coconut oil

1 cup butternut squash, cubed

2 garlic cloves, minced

½ cup nutritional yeast

½ tsp salt

¼ tsp freshly ground black pepper

Freshly ground nutmeg, to taste

Directions

1. Place cashews in a small saucepan and cover with water. Place saucepan over high heat and bring just to a boil. Cover, remove saucepan from heat and let sit for 15 minutes. Drain, rinse well, and place in a blender along with ½ cup broth. Puree until creamy and smooth.
2. In a medium saucepan, warm oil over medium heat. Add butternut squash and cook, stirring often until tender, about 8 minutes. Add garlic and cook until fragrant, about 30 seconds.
3. Stir in cashew cream, remaining ½ cup broth, nutritional yeast, salt, pepper, and nutmeg. Bring to a simmer while stirring and let cook for 3–5 minutes.
4. Transfer back to blender, and blend until very smooth. If sauce is too thick, adjust its consistency with some extra broth or water. Adjust seasoning with additional salt, pepper, and nutmeg.

Tip: This sauce is delicious swirled into cooked pasta or zoodles, but it is equally at home draped over steamed or roasted vegetables.

It is great dipped into crackers or tortilla chips, but as a sauce it is delicious swirled into spiralized veggies or your favorite pasta (or as a layer in the *Roasted Vegetable Lasagna* on page 241), and is equally at home draped over steamed or roasted vegetables.

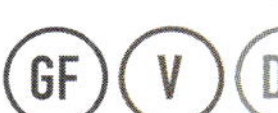

Vegan Marinara Meatballs

The first time I made these "meatballs" for my family, I made them all try to guess what the "meat" was. Even my Italian husband couldn't believe they were from lentils and chickpeas. When I am really changing ingredients and using a lot of healthy ones, I sometimes wait until after my family tells me they like it... then I let them in on my little secrets. Anyone else do that?

Servings: *4–6*	**Prep time:** *25 mins*	**Cook time:** *20 mins*

Ingredients

1½ Tbsp flax, ground

4½ Tbsp water

⅓ cup pumpkin seeds, raw

½ cup old fashioned oats

2 cups canned lentils, drained and rinsed

1 cup canned chickpeas, drained and rinsed

½ cup onion, diced

3 garlic clove, minced, divided

1½ tsp Italian dried herb blend

1 tsp salt, divided

½ tsp ground black pepper

¼ cup fresh basil leaves (optional)

1 Tbsp grapeseed oil

1 (28 oz) can crushed tomatoes

1 tsp coconut sugar

1 tsp basil, dried

¼ tsp hot red pepper flakes, crushed (optional)

Directions

1. Preheat oven to 375 °F (190 °C).
2. In a small bowl stir, together flax and water. Set aside to thicken up while making meatball mixture.
3. In a food processor, pulse pumpkin seeds and oats until finely ground. Add lentils, chickpeas, onion, 1 minced garlic clove, Italian herb blend, ½ tsp salt, pepper, and basil leaves, if using.
4. Pulse until everything is well combined, but still slightly chunky. Add flax mixture and pulse until well incorporated.
5. With slightly wet hands, roll heaping spoonfuls of mixture into balls before placing on a parchment-lined baking tray. You should have about 12 golf ball-sized meatballs. Bake, flipping once halfway through baking time, until lightly browned, about 15–20 minutes total.
6. While meatballs bake, heat oil in a large skillet over medium-low heat. Add remaining 2 minced garlic cloves and cook until fragrant and starting to brown, about 2 minutes. Stir in tomatoes, remaining ½ tsp salt, sugar, basil, and chili flakes, if using. Allow sauce to come to a low simmer and, stirring occasionally, let sauce cook for about 8 minutes.
7. Add cooked meatballs to sauce and let cook for 8–10 minutes over low heat. Serve over noodles, in a sandwich or on their own.

Linguini with Clams

When my husband and I travel to Italy, we eat pasta, and a lot of it (insert happiness, lol). And my favorites include a simple Pomodoro, and pasta vongole (clams). Especially in Rome, and the southern party of Italy, pasta vongole is always served in a simple white sauce with fresh parsley. Back on the West Coast, I make a simple sauce, but I also add a few cherry or grape tomatoes for a touch of flavor.

Servings: *4+*	**Prep time:** *10 mins**	**Cook time:** *10 mins*

Ingredients

1 lb manila clams (soaked in cold salted water for about 30 minutes to help remove sand, change water once)

1 Tbsp butter

3 Tbsp olive oil

1 small leek, thinly sliced and well washed

¼ cup chicken broth

¼ cup dry white wine

½ tsp sea salt

½ cup cherry tomatoes

3 cloves garlic, sliced

Pinch of red pepper flakes

½ cup fresh parsley, chopped

1 lb linguine (or your favorite pasta)

Directions

1. Bring a large pot of salted water to a boil. Cook pasta according to package directions.
2. In a large skillet on stove, over medium heat, add butter, olive oil, leeks. Cook for approximately 3–5 minutes or until leeks are translucent and fragrant. Add sliced garlic and sauté for another 2 minutes.
3. Squeeze the juice of cherry tomatoes into skillet and add the remaining tomato into pan. Let tomato soften and get incorporated into butter and olive oil, about 5 minutes.
4. Add broth, wine, (if using), sea salt, red pepper flakes.
5. Add clams.
6. Cover with a tight lid, and keep on a gentle simmer. Cook until clams start to open. Stir occasionally. Once clams are completely opened, they're ready. Remove from skillet and transfer to a bowl. Shuck some of the clams, leaving some in their shell. Those clams that don't open should be discarded.
7. While clams are out of skillet, add parsley and let simmer about 5 minutes. Return clams to pan.
8. Once pasta is ready, drain, and add to clams until well combined.
9. Serve with a glass of pinot grigio and additional red pepper flakes and parsley as garnish.

*Plus time for clams to soak

Tip: This dish cooks so simply and is ready once the clams have opened. Look for smaller clams (manila clams) at your local fish monger or grocery store.

Turkey Quinoa Meatloaf

How many of you ate meatloaf as kids? Growing up on a farm, we were definitely a meat and potato kind of family, and meatloaf was a regular eat. I wanted a meatloaf that is packed with flavor, but also nutrition, and this turkey meatloaf is all of that. Moist, delicious, and nutritious, it uses quinoa as the secret stuffing to give it extra fiber.

Servings: *6+*	**Prep time:** *15 mins + time for quinoa*	**Cook time:** *1 h*

Ingredients

½ cup cooked quinoa (cook according to package directions)

1¼ lb turkey, ground

1 onion, diced

¼ cup fresh parsley, chopped

2 garlic clove, minced

½ tsp salt

¼ tsp black pepper

½ tsp oregano

¼ cup whole wheat panko breadcrumbs

1 large egg, lightly beaten

1 tsp extra virgin olive oil

Splash of milk

Jar of marinara sauce, or you can make your own found on page 251 (vegan meatball with marinara sauce)

6 fresh basil leaves

Directions

1. Cook quinoa according to package directions. Let it cool down completely.
2. Preheat oven to 375 °F (190 °C). Grease a loaf pan with extra virgin olive oil.
3. In a large bowl, place turkey, seasonings, cooled quinoa, bread crumbs, egg, and mix together with hands. Make sure it's well combined.
4. Transfer meat to prepared loaf pan. Smooth meat with back of spoon.
5. Pour marinara sauce on the meat.
6. Cover with foil and bake for about 45 minutes. Remove cover the last 15 minutes or so for it to brown. Check internal temperature with thermometer to make sure it's well done (165 °F/75 °C).
7. 5 minutes before you remove from oven sprinkle fresh basil leaves

Tip: You could make this with ground beef as well, but I love turkey as it's a lean source of protein. I also love adding chopped cooked spinach for additional greens

Oven-Roasted Chicken & Vegetables

One of my favorite Sunday dinners is oven-roasted chicken. It's actually such a quick, simple, and flavorful way to cook chicken. We are a two-chicken family now, as I love extra meat for soup, sandwiches, and pasta. I always make chicken stock out of the leftover carcass, so every piece of this gets used. As per my recommendations in the first chapter, I highly suggest an organic, grass-fed chicken to yield higher amounts of healthy fats and quality protein.

Servings: *4*	**Prep time:** *20 mins*	**Cook time:** *1½ h*

Ingredients

1 whole organic chicken (about 5 lb)

1 Tbsp butter

1 Tbsp extra virgin olive oil

1 lemon cut into wedges

3 garlic cloves

1 tsp sea salt

½ tsp garlic powder

½ cup chicken stock (or dry white wine)

Fresh herbs such as thyme and rosemary

Fall vegetables

- ½ lb fresh baby potatoes
- 2 parsnips
- 4 large carrots
- 2 whole yellow onions quartered

Directions

1. Preheat oven to 375 °F (190 °C).
2. Wash chicken thoroughly and pat dry.
3. Set aside in your roasting pan while you prepare the vegetables.
4. Wash and peel vegetables. Cut into desired size. Place in a bowl and drizzle with 1 tablespoon olive oil, a pinch of sea salt, and cracked pepper. Toss until well coated.
5. Place vegetables around the chicken.
6. Prepare chicken by using a basting brush to distribute olive oil and butter to coat the chicken. Sprinkle all seasonings on top.
7. Place fresh herbs on top and inside chicken cavity.
8. Place lemon wedges and garlic cloves inside the chicken.
9. Tie the legs of chicken with butcher's string.
10. Place in oven and roast until meat thermometer says it's cooked, approximately 1½ hours. I usually baste it once or twice during roasting process with pan juices.
11. Turn vegetables partway through and remove once fork-tender. Set aside.
12. Once roasted, let sit on cutting board for 10 minutes before carving.

Tip: To make a complete meal even easier, I will often add my vegetables right into the roasting pan (I usually remove the vegetables before the chicken is roasted so as not to overcook them).

Lamb Shank Curry

Once a week, usually on Sundays, I prepare a heartier dinner, and most often meat is involved. Lamb is one of my favorites, and it was actually the first meat I gave to my kids when they were babies as it's the most hypoallergenic of all. I have learned to cook lamb from my mother-in-law, as it's most definitely part of the Italian cuisine. There are so many ways to prepare lamb, but I find grilling, or slow cooking to yield the most flavorful and tender meat.

Servings: *4*	**Prep time:** *20 mins*	**Cook time:** *8 h (in slow cooker)*

Ingredients

2 Tbsp grapeseed oil

1 large yellow onion, chopped

6 Tbsp plain yogurt, divided

½ cup vegetable stock or water

1 tsp sea salt

2 Tbsp tomato paste

1 Tbsp ginger, minced

2 garlic cloves, minced

½ tsp chili powder

2 tsp cumin, ground

2 tsp coriander, ground

1 tsp turmeric, ground

¼ tsp cardamom, ground

4 lamb shanks (about 3 lb), washed and patted dry with paper towel

Directions

1. Heat oil in a frying pan over medium heat. Add onions and cook, stirring often, until softened and golden brown, about 10–12 minutes. Transfer onions to a slow cooker along with ¼ cup yogurt, stock, salt, and tomato paste. Stir to combine.
2. In a large bowl stir together remaining 2 tablespoons yogurt, ginger, garlic, chili powder, cumin, coriander, turmeric, and cardamom until a paste forms. Add lamb shanks and coat in spice paste. Transfer spice covered shanks to slow cooker, cover, and turn on low for 8 hours. Lamb shanks should be fork-tender.

Tip: This recipe uses the slow cooker, and is a great dish to prepare early on a Sunday morning and then head out for a day of Sunday Funday with the family, to return home and find your home filled with the delicious and hearty aroma of Sunday dinner. Serve alongside rice, mashed, roasted potatoes or along with any sauce over steamed rice, if desired.

SWEET TREATS

Do you favor sweet or savory? Admittedly I have a strong penchant for the sweet, for me it kind of seals the deal at the end of hearty meal. I don't need a lot, but just a little, and even a square of dark chocolate will satisfy. That's because I have re-trained my taste buds to what sweet actually tastes like. It wasn't always like this back in the 90s as I was a sugar/carb lover. Sugary drinks, white sugar used in everything (I don't even buy white sugar any longer), and large pieces of dessert were part of my jam. I later realized if I wanted to feel my best, I would have to cut the sweet and develop my taste buds to savor fresh strawberries as a treat. The best news I have, it is possible to have your cake and eat it too.

This chapter is filled with some of my most decadent, "sweet", yet unbelievably healthy desserts. Spelt, coconut, almond flours, along with dates, maple syrup, and coconut sugar make the basis of these yummy sweet treats. In fact they're so good for you, you could eat them for breakfast.

My favorite are the coconut flour donuts and beet brownies, but then again, that cashew frosting can be eaten by the spoonful.

I hope you find a place in your week to enjoy some of these sweet treats. Just remember that part of being healthy is enjoying life and the food you eat. May these treats bring health and happiness.

Lavender Latte

Lavender helps calm, soothe, and relax your mind and body. I love lavender in the bath, on my skin, diffused, and consumed in a latte. You can buy dried lavender flowers in most natural health shops.

Servings: *2*	**Prep time:** *5 mins*	**Cook time:** *10 mins*

Ingredients

1 cup full-fat coconut milk

1 cup boiling water

1 Tbsp coconut oil

2 Medjool dates, pitted

¼ tsp vanilla extract

½ tsp lavender flower, dried

Directions

1. Blend all the ingredients in a blender.
2. Reheat on medium heat for 5 minutes.
3. Serve in your favorite mug and top it off with dried lavender flower.

Warming Turmeric Milk

My mom used to make us warm milk with a spoonful of honey at bedtime. The theory was that it would help relax our bodies and help us sleep. All these years later, I'm still doing this, only now using coconut milk and turmeric powder. Besides a cup of peppermint tea, this is my go-to bedtime drink, and honestly I'm obsessed with the healing powers of turmeric morning, noon, and night. It's actually one of the nutrients I supplement with daily, and will continue to do so.

Servings: *2*	**Prep time:** *5 mins*	**Cook time:** *10 mins*

Ingredients

2 cups full-fat coconut milk

1 tsp turmeric powder
(or use fresh turmeric root)

1 tsp ginger, grated

1 Tbsp local honey

Pinch of black pepper

Pinch of cinnamon

Directions

1. Pour all the ingredients into a small saucepan and bring to a light boil. Reduce heat to low and simmer for up to 10 minutes.
2. To serve, strain the milk and enjoy it warm.

Tip: Add extra honey or cinnamon when serving.

For a complete list of my daily supplements and recommended brands see page 292.

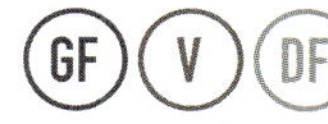

Chocolate Iced Vanilla Spiced Donut

Move over cupcakes, healthy donuts are the new sweet treat in town. You won't believe how delicious and healthy these donuts are. Baked, not fried; coconut flour and sugar, rather than white flour, sugar, and hydrogenated oils; iced with a sweet, chocolate creamy cashew frosting! These will be a crowd pleaser at your next gathering, including kids' birthday parties, as well as friends and family dinner parties. You will definitely want to double or triple your batch!

Servings: *9*	**Prep time:** *10 mins**	**Cook time:** *40 mins (bake & glaze)*

Ingredients

½ cup coconut flour

½ cup coconut sugar

1 tsp cream of tartar

½ tsp baking soda

¼ tsp salt

2 tsp cinnamon, ground

¼ tsp nutmeg, ground

1 tsp cardamom, ground

6 eggs, lightly beaten

¼ cup avocado oil or melted coconut oil

2½ tsp vanilla extract, divided

1 cup raw cashews,
*soaked in water at least 4 hours and drained

¼ cup maple syrup

⅓ cup almond milk or other milk of choice

2 Tbsp raw cacao powder

½ cup toasted coconut ribbons

Directions

1. Preheat over to 350 °F (175 °C). Grease your donut pan well with extra avocado oil. The number of donut pans you will use will depend on the quantity each donut cavity holds.
2. Sift coconut flour into a large bowl before whisking in coconut sugar, cream of tartar, baking soda, salt, cinnamon, nutmeg, and cardamom. Make a well in the center of the dry ingredients and add the eggs, oil, and 2 teaspoons vanilla extract.
3. With a wooden spoon stir batter together until well combined. Spoon into prepared donut pan and bake until a wooden toothpick inserted in a donut comes out clean, about 15–18 minutes.
4. Let donuts cool in pan for 10 minutes before turning out onto a wire cooling rack to cool completely at room temperature.
5. While donuts cool, make chocolate icing. In a blender, combine drained cashews with remaining ½ tsp vanilla extract, maple syrup, almond milk, and cacao powder until smooth.
6. Once donuts have cooled completely, spread with icing and garnish with a sprinkling of toasted coconut ribbons, if desired. These donuts are best served within a couple of hours of assembling.

Chocolate-Almond Butter Cups

These chocolate almond butter cups are inspired by my love of *Reese* peanut butter cups. When comes Halloween, even my boys know, I will be picking out their peanut butter cups. However, these ones are so much better for you (and just as tasty) and can be eaten completely guilt free.

Servings: *12*	**Prep time:** *10 mins*	**Cook time:** *1 h (to set)*

Ingredients

½ cup raw cacao powder

½ cup coconut oil

½ cup pure maple syrup

Pinch of Himalayan salt

1 tsp vanilla extract

4 Tbsp runny almond butter

Sea salt, for topping

Directions

1. In a double boiler, add the cacao powder, coconut oil, and maple syrup. Once it's melted and well mixed, remove from the heat.
2. Pour approximately 1 teaspoon of the chocolate mixture in the bottom of each cup, followed by ½ teaspoon almond butter, and then topped with another teaspoon of the chocolate mixture.
3. Sprinkle with sea salt. Put the chocolate cups on a flat tray into the fridge to set for about 1 hour.
4. Enjoy them with a cup of tea or as a desert /snack.

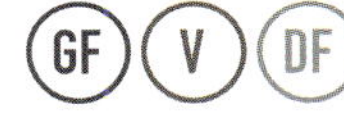

Chocolate-Raspberry Chia Cups

These chocolate raspberry cups make a healthy sweet treat, and because they are nut free, they are also a great choice for kids' parties or to send to school. They are simple to make and the sauce can be made with raspberries, blueberries, or strawberries. The chia seeds in the jam provide healthy fiber, protein, and omega-3s, making these a nourishing treat to enjoy anytime.

Servings: *6*	**Prep time:** *15 mins*	**Cook time:** *15 mins*

Ingredients

Raspberry-chia jam

- 1 cup fresh raspberries
- 1 Tbsp coconut nectar or maple syrup
- 1 Tbsp chia seeds
- ½ tsp vanilla

Chocolate cups

- 2 cups dark chocolate chips (or equivalent amount of your favorite dark chocolate)
- 2 Tbsp coconut oil

Directions *(raspberry-chia jam)*

1. In a small saucepan over medium heat, add raspberries and let soften.
2. Add the maple syrup and vanilla; continue to cook over low-medium heat. Keep stirring.
3. A sauce will start to form. Once it's runny, remove from heat and stir in chia seeds. Set aside and let gel (and cool) about 10 minutes.

Directions *(chocolate cups)*

1. Line a muffin tin with either *Slipat* liners or paper liners.
2. Using a double boiler melt 1 cup of chocolate, and 1 tablespoon coconut oil. Continue stirring chocolate until melted; do not let chocolate burn.
3. Add 1 tablespoon of chocolate to each liner. Place in freezer for about 10 minutes.
4. Once settled place 1 teaspoon of jam in center of each chocolate cup.
5. Prepare second batch of chocolate. Once ready add 1 tablespoon of chocolate on top of jam.
6. Return to freezer for 10 minutes or until hardened.

Apple-Pear Quinoa Crumble

Baked fruit with a layer of topping, yes please. There are so many names for these types of desserts, crisp, crumble, or cobbler, all with slight variations on the ingredients used to prepare. They are like a deconstructed pie, and are much easier to assemble as there is less rolling and precision required. They are also very nourishing when made with healthy ingredients such as quinoa, oats, coconut, and almond flour. There are so many options for the fruit used.

Servings: *6*	**Prep time:** *20 mins*	**Cook time:** *40 mins*

Ingredients

3 pears, core removed and sliced

2 honey crisps apples, core removed and chopped

¼ cup coconut sugar

2 cups cooked quinoa

1 cup quinoa flakes

¼ almond flour

¼ cup chopped pistachio

½ tsp cinnamon

¼ cup coconut oil

¼ cup maple syrup

Crisp: A baked fruit dessert topped with a crisp and crunchy layer of ingredients. The dessert is baked just until the topping is crisp and golden.

Crumble: Similar to a crisp, a crumble is a baked fruit dessert with a layer of topping. The topping is generally more clumpy than a crisp topping, but not as clumpy as a cobbler topping.

Cobbler: A cobbler is a deep-dish baked fruit dessert with a thick dropped-biscuit or pie-dough topping. Traditionally the rich fruit stew is the base for the topping, but variations can include the biscuits on the bottom, similar to a deep-dish pie. The common belief is that the name came from the biscuit topping's resemblance to cobblestones.

Directions

1. Preheat oven to 350 °F (175 °C). Grease a 9-inch cast iron with coconut oil and set aside.
2. In a small bowl, combine apples, pear, and coconut sugar.
3. In a large bowl, combine cooked quinoa, quinoa flakes, almond flour, pistachio, maple syrup, coconut oil, and cinnamon. Using a wooden spoon or your hands combine all these ingredients until a crumb texture is formed.
4. Toss in the apple and pear with the quinoa mixture.
5. Bake for 40 minutes, or until the top is brown and fruits are soft.
6. Enjoy warm with a scoop of vanilla ice cream!

Chocolate-Raspberry Cheesecake

If you're a cheesecake lover, this is the ultimate dessert and I can't speak enough about the crunchy cashew base which could actually be used for so many other desserts. You can sub in the non-dairy cream cheese for the regular cream cheese if you prefer. This is the perfect dessert to serve your guests or for a Sunday dinner treat. It looks fantastic topped with any type of fruit or berries. The drizzle of chocolate adds a decadent and gorgeous finish.

Servings: *12*	**Prep time:** *20 mins**	**Cook time:** *4 h to refrigerate*

Ingredients

1½ cups raw almonds or raw cashews

2 soft Medjool dates, pitted

¼ cup + 1 Tbsp cocoa powder, divided

2 Tbsp maple syrup or light agave syrup

¼ cup coconut oil, melted, divided

¾ cup raw cashews,
*soaked in water for 4 h and drained

½ cup coconut nectar (or agave if you prefer)

¼ cup coconut butter, at room temperature

¼ cup lemon juice

1 tsp vanilla extract

Pinch of salt

2 containers *Daiya* plain cream cheese style spread, at room temperature

1 tsp lemon zest, finely grated

1½ tsp water

3 cups fresh raspberries (or blueberries)

Directions

1. Rub a little coconut oil on inside surfaces of an 8-inch springform pan. Line bottom and sides of pan with parchment paper and set aside.
2. To make crust, in a food processor pulse together almonds, dates, and ¼ cup cocoa powder until almonds are coarsely ground. Add maple syrup and 2 tablespoons coconut oil before processing until mixture is well combined and holds together. Transfer to prepared springform pan and press into an even layer covering the base. Refrigerate while making filling.
3. To make filling, in a blender, mix together soaked cashews, coconut nectar, coconut mana, lemon juice, vanilla extract, and salt. Scrape down sides of blender as needed until mixture is very creamy and smooth. Remove 2 tablespoons of mixture to a small bowl and set aside.
4. Transfer remaining cashew mixture to a large bowl along with cream cheese style spread, lemon zest, and remaining 2 tablespoons coconut oil. Using a whisk or hand mixer fitted with whisk attachment, whisk mixture until well combined.
5. Pour into springform pan over crust and smooth top. Refrigerate for at least 4 hours.
6. To make chocolate topping, stir remaining 1 tablespoon cocoa powder and water into reserved cashew mixture. If chocolate topping is too thick to drizzle, add extra water ½ teaspoon at a time until desired consistency is achieved. Set aside at room temperature until ready to use.
7. About one hour before serving cheesecake, remove from pan, transfer to a serving plate and discard parchment paper. Cover top with a layer of raspberries before drizzling with chocolate topping. Refrigerate until ready to serve.

Blueberry Scones

A scone is in-between a cookie and a cake, and is a perfect accompaniment to tea time or a lazy weekend brunch. I love to eat them warm with jam, and my *Raspberry-chia jam* on page 269 make a unicorn couple – perfection! This recipe offers a healthy variation on a traditional scone by using coconut oil and coconut milk along with whole wheat flour.

Servings: *8*	**Prep time:** *20 mins*	**Cook time:** *15–18 mins*

Ingredients

2 cups whole wheat flour

½ cup organic white sugar

1 tsp baking powder

½ tsp baking soda

Pinch of sea salt

1 cup cold coconut oil, not melted

1 cup full-fat coconut milk

½ cup fresh blueberries

Directions

1. Preheat the oven to 400°F (205 °C).
2. In a large bowl, mix the whole wheat flour, sugar, baking powder, baking soda, and salt.
3. Add the cold coconut oil and combine with a pastry cutter or your fingers.
4. Add in the coconut milk and vanilla extract and mix to form dough, and then fold in the blueberries.
5. Transfer the dough onto a well-floured surface and shape into an 8-inch disc.
6. Slice into 8 triangles and arrange them on a baking tray lined with parchment paper.
7. Bake for 15–18 minutes. Check at 15 minutes and if the top is slightly golden brown and the corners are crisp, they are ready.

GF V DF

Raspberry Muffins

Take your favorite berry and turn them into muffin delight. These moist and nourishing lemon, raspberry muffins make me feel so happy. The lemon zest gives them such a bright and refreshing flavor. They will be on weekend repeat during berry season.

Servings: *12*	**Prep time:** *15 mins*	**Cook time:** *20–25 mins*

Ingredients

1½ cup gluten-free flour blend

1½ tsp baking powder

½ tsp baking soda

2 Tbsp flaxseeds + 6 Tbsp warm water (for flax eggs)

¼ cup melted coconut oil

¾ cup honey (the runny kind)

⅓ cup apple sauce

¾ cup coconut milk

1 cup frozen raspberries (may also use fresh raspberries)

Directions

1. Preheat oven to 350 °F (175 °C). Spray a muffin pan with coconut oil and set aside.
2. In a medium bowl, mix the flaxseeds with water and set aside for 10 minutes.
3. In a large bowl, combine the dry ingredients: flour, baking powder, and baking soda.
4. Once the flax eggs are ready, in the same bowl, add the melted coconut oil, honey, applesauce, coconut milk, and stir to combine.
5. Pour in the liquid mixture into the dry ingredients and mix gently to combine the ingredients well.
6. Stir in the raspberries.
7. Pour into a muffin pan about ¾ full.
8. Bake for 20–25 minutes at 350 °F or until the top is slightly golden.
9. Remove from the oven and allow to cool in the pan for 20 minutes.
10. Gently remove the muffins from the pan and transfer to a cooling rack for another 5 minutes before serving.

GF V DF

Carrot Cake with Creamy Cashew Frosting

Who remembers those large carrot cakes baked in a sheet pan covered in a layer of thick cream cheese icing. Oh so good. This recipe delivers all the flavor, but is so much healthier for you with the addition of spelt flour, maple syrup, and coconut oil.

Servings: *24*	**Prep time:** *20 mins*	**Cook time:** *1 h*

Ingredients

1 cup maple syrup

¾ cup melted coconut oil

3 eggs

1½ cup spelt flour

Pinch salt

1½ tsp baking soda

2 tsp cinnamon

½ tsp ginger, ground

½ cup unsweetened coconut, shredded

4 cups carrots, grated

½ cup raisins

Chopped pecans or walnuts (optional topping)

Cashew frosting

- 1 cup raw cashews, soaked
- Juice of 1 lemon (about ¼ cup)
- 2 Tbsp honey
- 3 Tbsp almond milk
- 1 tsp vanilla extract
- Pinch of salt

Traditional cream cheese frosting

- 1 block of cream cheese (room temp)
- 1 tsp vanilla extract
- 2–3 Tbsp butter
- A dash of milk
- Add powdered sugar until smooth

Directions

1. Preheat oven to 325 °F (165 °C); grease sides of 9 x 13-inch pan.
2. In a large bowl, beat together maple syrup, coconut oil, and eggs.
3. In a medium bowl, combine dry ingredients.
4. Add dry to wet ingredients and mix until combined.
5. Pour into the greased pan.
6. Bake for 1 hour or until toothpick inserted in the middle comes out clean.
7. While baking make the creamy cashew frosting (or alternative you could make a cream cheese frosting).
8. Let cake cool completely before smoothing frosting. Sprinkle cinnamon and chopped walnuts or pecans.

Directions *(cashew frosting)*

1. Meanwhile, make the icing by combining all of the ingredients in a high-speed blender and blend until smooth. Add additional almond milk in order to thin out the frosting and adjust the sweetness as desired.

Directions *(traditional frosting)*

1. Beat block of cream cheese with vanilla, butter, and milk. Add powdered sugar until desired sweetness and consistency is reached.
2. Spread on top of carrot cake once cooled.

Beet Brownies

Ooey, gooey, fudgy, rich, and decadent, you will not even believe there are beets inside these moist brownies. The beets allow you to cut down on the amount of oil while delivering a moist and nutritious treat. You will never want to make brownies any other way again.

Servings: *9*	**Prep time:** *15 mins*	**Cook time:** *55 mins*

Ingredients

Beet brownies

- 3 Tbsp flaxseeds + 9 Tbsp water
- 3 medium beets, cooked and chopped
- 1¼ cup almond flour
- ½ cup cacao powder, raw and unsweetened
- 1 tsp baking powder
- ½ tsp baking soda
- ½ tsp salt
- 1 tsp cinnamon
- ¼ cup coconut oil, melted
- ¾ cup full-fat coconut milk
- ¾ cup maple syrup
- Chopped hazelnuts, enough for the topping

Chocolate sauce topping

- ¼ cup cacao powder
- ¼ cup maple syrup
- ¼ coconut oil
- Pinch of sea salt
- 1 tsp vanilla extract

Directions

1. In a small bowl, mix together the flaxseeds and water. Set aside for 15 minutes to form a gel.
2. Preheat the oven to 375° F (190 °C). Lightly oil an 8 x 8-inch baking dish and set aside.
3. Using a food processor or a blender, puree the beets.
4. Add the remaining ingredients (almond flour, cacao powder, baking powder, baking soda, salt, cinnamon, coconut oil, coconut milk, maple syrup, and flaxseed gel) to the food processor/blender. Mix well until completely smooth.
5. Pour the brownie batter into the prepared baking dish and smooth it evenly. Place on the center rack of the oven and bake for 45–55 minutes. (Check at 45 minutes and insert a tooth pick in the center, if it comes out clean it's ready).
6. Meanwhile prepare the chocolate topping by mixing the cacao powder, maple syrup, coconut oil, sea salt, and vanilla extract in a saucepan over medium heat. Heat for 3–4 minutes while mixing. The final result should look like chocolate sauce.
7. Allow brownies to cool for 30 minutes before topping them with chocolate sauce and chopped hazelnuts. Slice into squares and serve right away.
8. Store the leftovers in the refrigerator for up to a week. They also freeze very well for up to a month, and can be reheated.

Olive Oil Peach Cake

Out of all the recipes in the book, this is the one that I had to keep redoing, over and over again to get it just right. It worked perfectly with all-purpose flour, but as soon as I switched to a more dense/nourishing flour it would implode in the middle (I almost wanted to cry, or maybe I even did, haha). But then I got it right, and now this is one of my favorite cakes to serve in the summer. This is delicious topped with whipping cream or iced cream.

Servings: *8*	**Prep time:** *20 mins*	**Cook time:** *45 mins*

Ingredients

1½ cup whole wheat flour

1 cup almond flour

1 cup coconut sugar

½ tsp baking powder

½ tsp baking soda

¼ tsp salt

3 eggs

¼ cup of extra virgin olive oil

¼ cup maple syrup

1 cup unsweetened almond milk

3 peaches, peeled and thinly sliced

Organic powdered sugar, enough for the topping

Directions

1. Preheat the oven to 350 °F (175 °C). Grease sides and bottom of a 9-inch springform cake pan with cooking oil. Line the bottom of the pan with parchment paper and make sure to grease the top of parchment as well.
2. In a medium bowl, combine the whole wheat flour, almond flour, coconut sugar, baking powder, baking soda, and salt.
3. In a small bowl, whisk the 3 eggs with olive oil, maple syrup, and almond milk.
4. Gradually add liquid mixture to the dry ingredients and mix until there are no lumps.
5. Pour the batter into the prepared pan. Arrange peach slices on top of batter in a single, even layer with a little space between each.
6. Place the cake pan in the oven and bake for about 40–45 minutes, or until toothpick or fork come out clean and the middle is set. Cool the cake on wire rack for 30 minutes before serving.
7. When cool, carefully remove side of pan. Serve with a sprinkle of powdered sugar and maybe a scoop of coconut whip cream.
8. Enjoy!

Tip: Sub in any berry or other tree fruit (apricots, nectarines, or plums would also work well).

Pumpkin Ginger Loaf

This recipe will be on repeat from October to the end of December as it combines all the festive fall flavors and aromas. Loafs are so great for serving at brunch or when your besties come over for coffee. This recipe is also school safe and makes a great snack to send in the kids' lunch box.

Servings: *10*	**Prep time:** *20 mins*	**Cook time:** *50 mins*

Ingredients

1¾ cup spelt flour

1 cup coconut sugar

1 Tbsp cinnamon

½ tsp nutmeg

½ tsp cloves

1 tsp baking soda

½ tsp baking powder

Pinch of sea salt

2 eggs

1 cup pumpkin puree, unsweetened

¼ cup almond milk

¼ cup melted coconut oil

2 Tbsp fresh ginger, minced

¼ cup dry cranberries

¼ cup pumpkin seeds

Directions

1. Preheat oven to 350 °F (175 °C); lightly grease a medium loaf pan and set aside.
2. In a large mixing bowl, mix together spelt flour, coconut sugar, cinnamon, nutmeg, cloves, baking soda, baking powder, and salt.
3. In a medium bowl, beat the eggs; mix in the pumpkin puree, almond milk, melted coconut oil, and ginger.
4. Transfer this mixture to the dry ingredients bowl and combine until all ingredients are mixed.
5. Fold in the cranberries and pumpkin seeds.
6. Transfer the batter in the prepared loaf pan and bake for 50 minutes or until a toothpick comes out clean.
7. Let cool completely before serving.
8. Spread with your favorite butter, or just enjoy on its own with a cup of tea or coffee.

Raspberry-Chia Thumbprint Cookies

These cookies are so sweet and festive especially around the holidays, when cut using your favorite cookie cutter. You could also make these at Thanksgiving/Halloween using pumpkin puree and a drizzle of chocolate overtop, or the *Peach-Apricot Chia Jam* (recipe found on page 65) If I'm in a hurry I also just drop spoonfuls of the dough onto a cookie sheet and let bake without forming into shapes.

Servings: *12*	**Prep time:** *15 mins*	**Cook time:** *12–14 mins + cooling time*

Ingredients

1 cup spelt flour

½ cup + 3 Tbsp oat flour

⅓ cup almond flour

⅓ cup coconut oil, melted

¼ cup + 3 Tbsp maple syrup

Raspberry-chia jam for the topping (See recipe on page 269)

More oat flour (to cover the counter)

Directions

1. Preheat the oven to 320° F (160 °C). Cover a baking tray with parchment paper and set aside.
2. In a medium bowl, combine all the ingredients and mix until sticky dough forms.
3. Cover the top of your counter with some oat flour and roll your mixture out until it's perfectly smooth and the thickness is about ¼ inch.
4. Use a heart-shaped cookie cutter to cut shapes and transfer to a baking tray (you will have to roll the dough a few time to get the most out of it).
5. Once you cut all the cookies, press a thumbprint into the center of each heart (this is where the jam goes after the cookies are baked).
6. Transfer your baking tray into the oven and bake for 12–14 minutes (until the edges are golden brown).
7. Once the cookies are baked, let them cool completely on a cooling rack.
8. Now it's time to fill in the middle with some raspberry-chia jam.

Peanut Butter Chocolate Cookies

Peanut butter cookies and a glass of milk, all grown up. Nourishing and protein-rich flours like oat and almond combined with natural peanut butter make these cookies healthy enough for breakfast or a filling snack.

Servings: *12*	**Prep time:** *10 mins*	**Cook time:** *14 mins*

Ingredients

1 cup oat flour

1 cup almond flour

¼ tsp sea salt

½ tsp baking soda

½ tsp baking powder

2 tsp vanilla extract

½ cup natural peanut butter

¼ cup coconut milk

⅓ cup melted coconut oil

⅓ cup vegan chocolate chips
(I used 70% dark chocolate chips)

Directions

1. Preheat oven to 350° F (175 °C); line a baking tray with parchment paper and set aside.
2. In a large bowl, mix together the oat flour, almond flour, sea salt, baking soda, and baking powder.
3. Add the peanut butter, melted coconut oil, coconut milk, and vanilla extract to the flour mixture bowl and combine to form dough.
4. Fold in the chocolate chips. Using a cookie scooper or your hands form 2-inch balls. Place them on the baking tray and gently flat each cookie with the back of a fork.
5. Bake for 12–14 minutes, until the top is slightly brown.
6. Transfer to a cooling rack and allow to cool for 15 minutes before serving.
7. Enjoy!

Bird's Nest Cookies

These cookies are the heartiest, most complete, yet delicious cookie you will ever eat, no matter the name. It's a cookie you can feel good about feeding your family (or snacking on yourself). I love cookies with lots of nuts and seeds as they feel so satisfying. These cookies also freeze very well, so you might want to consider doubling your batch.

Servings: *14*	**Prep time:** *10 mins*	**Cook time:** *25 mins*

Ingredients

½ cup pumpkin puree

1 mashed banana

2 Tbsp almond butter

¼ cup unsweetened shredded coconut

4 dates, pitted and chopped

¼ cup flaxseeds

1 Tbsp chia seeds

½ cup natural almonds, well chopped

⅓ cup rolled oats

1 tsp vanilla extract

¼ tsp ground cinnamon

⅓ cup mini chocolate chips, optional

Directions

1. Preheat oven to 350 °F (175 °C). Line a large baking tray with parchment paper and set aside.
2. In a large bowl, stir together all ingredients with a wooden spoon until well combined. Roll 2 tablespoons of dough into a ball and on a prepared baking tray before gently flattening with the palm of your hand.
3. Repeat with remaining dough. Bake until golden brown, about 20–25 minutes. Transfer to a wire rack to cool completely.
4. Once cooled, cookies may be refrigerated in an airtight container for up to 1 week.

Summer Popsicles

Once the month of May hits, I go into popsicle overdrive. I absolutely love creating different variations of popsicles, and have given you a few of my favorite options here. You can even make extra smoothie in the morning and freeze the remainder into your popsicle mold. I use a stainless steel popsicle mold which gives them a vintage feel; I included my favorite one in the resource guide on page 292. You may never want to buy store-bought popsicles again.

Servings: *10*	**Prep time:** *10 mins*	**Cook time:** *Freeze overnight*

Tropical Popsicles

1 cup of tropical fruit blend
(I like pineapple, strawberry, and mango)

2 cup full-fat coconut milk

1 tsp vanilla extract

Pinch of salt

Directions

1. In a high-speed blender, blend all the ingredients until completely smooth.
2. Pure the mixture in to a popsicle mold.
3. Freeze for at least 4 hours or overnight.
4. When ready to serve, leave the popsicles mold on the counter for a few minutes for easier removal of the popsicles.

Avocado Mango Creamsicles

First layer

1 cup full-fat coconut milk

1 mango, skin removed and chopped into small pieces

1 Tbsp maple syrup

Second layer

1 medium avocado

½ cup full-fat coconut milk

½ tsp vanilla extract

¼ cup maple syrup

Pinch of salt

Directions

1. Combine the ingredients for the first layer and fill the popsicle mold with this mixture half way through.
2. Freeze for 15 minutes.
3. In a blender, combine the ingredients for the second layer. Next, fill up the remaining half of the popsicle mold. Cover with the lid and insert the sticks.
4. Allow to freeze for 6 hours or overnight.

Maple Strawberry & Cream Omega-3 Popsicles

1 lb strawberries, hulled and halved

5 Tbsp maple syrup or light agave syrup, divided

1 Tbsp lemon juice

1–2 Tbsp Sea-licious® Natural Maple Flavor

1½ cups coconut milk

1½ tsp vanilla extract

Directions

1. In a medium saucepan, stir together strawberries and 3 tablespoons maple syrup over medium heat. Cook, stirring occasionally, until soft and have released some juice, about 5 minutes. Remove from heat and stir in lemon juice. Set aside and allow to cool at room temperature.
2. Meanwhile, in a bowl or large measuring cup, whisk together coconut milk, remaining 2 table-spoons maple syrup and vanilla extract.
3. Once strawberry mixture has cooled, stir in Sea-licious Natural Maple Flavor (or you could use the Raspberry Lemonade, or Kids Cotton Candy flavor) before mashing mixture with a potato masher or a fork. Mixture should be well combined, but still a bit chunky, with small bits of fruit throughout.
4. Spoon a tablespoon of strawberry mixture into bottom of popsicle molds. Top with some of the cream mixture and continue layering until molds are evenly filled. Freeze for 30 minutes before placing a popsicle stick in the center of each mold. Continue freezing popsicles until set, at least 4 hours. Unmold popsicles and enjoy.

Chapter Seven

Resource Guide

My food journey has not only led me to appreciate the nourishment of delicious food, but also to find the beauty in creating the setting. I love beautiful pieces that enhance the gorgeousness of what food should taste and look like – from choosing beautiful linens and dishes to high-quality ingredients that bring out the best of the dish. These are some of my favorite things.

VegiDay™ Vegan Organic Protein
myvegiday.com

Natural Factors Whole Earth & Sea® Fermented Greens + Protein & Greens
naturalfactors.com

Sea-licious® Omega-3 oils
sealicious.ca

Alpha Health products, coconut oil, coconut blossom, and coconut flour
alphahealth.ca

La Tourangelle artisan oils and organic specialty cooking oils
latourangelle.com

Maison Orphee
Maisonorphee.com

Nuts to You (nut butters)
Nty.mi.ca

Cha's Organics (spices and canned coconut milk)
chasorganics.com

Simply Organic
Simplyorganic.com

Anita's Organic Mill
anitasorganic.com

Califia Organic
califiafarms.com

Blue Moon Organics
bluemoonorganics.com

Cosman & Webb Organic Maple Syrup
coswebb.ca

Olympic Dairy
olympicdairy.com

Fox Run Ice Pop Maker
amazon.ca

Cutco
Cutco.com

Vitamix
vitamix.ca

Le Creuset
lecreuset.ca

Kitchen Aid
kitchenaid.com

All Clad
all-clad.ca

Staub
Staub.com

Etsy Canada
Etsy.ca

Ikea
Ikea.com

Food52
food52.com/shop

Peridot Decorative Homewear
peridotdecorativehomewear.ca

Anthropologie
anthropologie.com

West Elm
westelm.com

Williams-Sonoma
williams-sonoma.com

The Cross Design
thecrossdesign.com

HomeSense
homesense.ca

Organizations

Environmental Working Group
ewg.org

Plant a Seed & See What Grows Foundation
seewhatgrows.org

Index

A

Almond butter
- Bird's Nest Cookies 289
- Breakfast Power Cookies 81
- Chocolate-Almond Butter Chia Pudding 63
- Chocolate-Almond Butter Cups 267
- Omega-3 Energy Balls 107
- Vanilla Pear & Almond-Baked Oatmeal 87

Almond milk
- Berry-Banana Oat Smoothie 57
- Berry Smoothie Bowl 59
- Carrot Cake with Creamy Cashew Frosting 277
- Chocolate-Almond Butter Chia Pudding 63
- Chocolate Iced Vanilla Spiced Donut 265
- Chocolate Peanut Butter Smoothie Bowl 59
- Corn Chowder 129
- Healthy Spelt Banana Bread 111
- Mango Strawberry Pre-Workout Smoothie 55
- Olive Oil Peach Cake 281
- Protein Banana Blender Pancakes 67
- Pumpkin Ginger Loaf 283
- Spicy Turmeric Cauliflower Tacos 215
- Vanilla Pear & Almond-Baked Oatmeal 87

Apple sauce
- Raspberry Muffins 275

Artichoke
- Artichokes 151
- Wheat Berry Quinoa Kale Salad 173

Avocado
- Avocado Dressing 161
- Avocado Mango Creamsicles 291
- Avocado Toast 91
- Mediterranean Quinoa Salad 169
- Slow Cooker Tortilla Soup 143
- Spicy Turmeric Cauliflower Tacos 215
- Strawberry, Fennel Salad & Lemony Chia Dressing 163
- The Best Guacamole 101
- Wheat Berry Quinoa Kale Salad 173

B

Banana
- Banana-Walnut Muffin 79
- Berry-Banana Oat Smoothie 57
- Bird's Nest Cookies 289
- Breakfast Power Cookies 81
- Chocolate Peanut Butter Smoothie Bowl 59
- Citrus & Greens Energizing Smoothie 55
- Green Tropical Smoothie 55
- Healing Turmeric Smoothie 56
- Healthy Spelt Banana Bread 111
- Protein Banana Blender Pancakes 67
- Smoothies – Nutrition in a Cup 53
- Tropical Granola 83

Beets
- Beet Brownies 279
- Orange Beet Kale Salad 155
- Roasted Golden Beet Hummus 103
- Wheat Berry Quinoa Kale Salad 173

Black beans
- Black Bean & Lentil Burgers 205
- Corn & Black Bean Salsa 153
- Slow Cooker Tortilla Soup 143
- Sweet & Spicy Turkey Chili 227

Blueberry
- Blueberry-Lemon Loaf with Yogurt Drizzle 113
- Blueberry Scones 274
- Lemon-Blueberry Waffles 73

Bocconcini
- Mediterranean Quinoa Salad 169

Brussels sprouts
- Creamy Parmesan Brussels Sprouts 183
- Wheat Berry Quinoa Kale Salad 173

Buckwheat flour
- Blueberry-Lemon Loaf with Yogurt Drizzle 113

Butter beans
- Creamy Butter Bean Dip 99

Butternut squash
- Butternut Squash Noodles with Pesto Chicken 223
- Cashew Butternut Squash Alfredo Sauce 249
- Roasted Butternut Squash 189
- Roasted Butternut Squash Soup 145

C

Cabbage
- Creamy Coleslaw with Lemon-Tahini Dressing 177
- Fish Taco 221
- Hearty Minestrone Soup 131

Cake
- Carrot Cake with Creamy Cashew Frosting 277
- Olive Oil Peach Cake 281

Carob powder
- Ricotta-Pumpkin Pancakes 71

Carrot
- Black Bean & Lentil Burgers 205
- Carrot-Apple Waffles 75
- Carrot Cake with Creamy Cashew Frosting 277
- Creamy Coleslaw with Lemon-Tahini Dressing 177
- Fish Taco 221
- Green Coconut Curry 213
- Hearty Black-Eyed Pea Kale Soup 127
- Hearty Minestrone Soup 131
- Hearty Rainbow Salad 157
- Lemony Lentil Soup 141
- Maple Turmeric Roasted Rainbow Carrots 191
- Massaged Kale Salad with Dijon-Lemon Dressing 165
- Morning Glory Muffins 77
- Oven-Roasted Chicken & Vegetables 257
- Peanut Butter Pasta 217
- Roasted Heirloom Tomato-Basil Soup 121
- Roasted Vegetable Lasagna 241
- Spiced Carrot-Turmeric Soup 125
- Tomato Lentil Soup 135
- Vegetable Stock 195

Cashews
- Carrot Cake with Creamy Cashew Frosting 277
- Cashew Butternut Squash Alfredo Sauce 249
- Cashew Cream Sauce 243
- Chocolate Iced Vanilla Spiced Donut 265
- Chocolate-Raspberry Cheesecake 273
- Creamy Vegan Caesar Dressing 159
- Cucumber Noodle Salad 171
- Fermented Cashew Dip 95
- Roasted Vegetable Lasagna 241
- Spicy Turmeric Cauliflower Tacos 215

Cauliflower
- Braised Cauliflower & Kale 239
- Cauliflower Tabouli 175
- Cauliflower Turmeric Soup 137
- Creamy Cauliflower Pasta Sauce 207
- Roasted Cauliflower with Hemp Seeds 193
- Spicy Turmeric Cauliflower Tacos 215

Celery
Hearty Black-Eyed Pea Kale Soup 127
Tuna Salad Wrap 203
Vegetable Stock 195
Cheesecake
Chocolate-Raspberry Cheesecake 273
Chia seed
Berry-Banana Oat Smoothie 57
Bird's Nest Cookies 289
Blueberry-Lemon Loaf with Yogurt Drizzle 113
Carrot-Apple Waffles 75
Chocolate-Almond Butter Chia Pudding 63
Chocolate Peanut Butter Smoothie Bowl 59
Chocolate-Raspberry Chia Cups 269
Citrus & Greens Energizing Smoothie 55
Omega-3 Energy Balls 107
Peach-Apricot Chia Jam 65
Protein Banana Blender Pancakes 67
Smoothies – Nutrition in a Cup 53
Strawberry, Fennel Salad & Lemony Chia Dressing 163
Chicken
Butternut Squash Noodles with Pesto Chicken 223
One-Pan Lemon Chicken Bake 225
Oven-Roasted Chicken & Vegetables 257
Slow Cooker Tortilla Soup 143
Weeknight Skillet Paella 235
Chickpeas
Oven-Roasted Chickpeas & Vegetables 201
Roasted Chickpeas 103
Roasted Red Pepper Hummus 105
Vegan Marinara Meatballs 251
Chocolate
Beet Brownies 279
Bird's Nest Cookies 289
Breakfast Power Cookies 81
Chocolate-Almond Butter Chia Pudding 63
Chocolate-Almond Butter Cups 267
Chocolate Iced Vanilla Spiced Donut 265
Chocolate Peanut Butter Smoothie Bowl 59
Chocolate-Raspberry Cheesecake 273
Chocolate-Raspberry Chia Cups 269
Chocolate Zucchini Loaf 115
Healthy Spelt Banana Bread 111
Morning Glory Muffins 77
Peanut Butter Chocolate Cookies 287
Coconut
Apple-Cinnamon Multigrain Pancakes 69
Avocado Mango Creamsicles 291
Beet Brownies 279
Berry-Banana Oat Smoothie 57
Berry Smoothie Bowl 59
Bird's Nest Cookies 289
Blueberry Scones 274
Breakfast Power Cookies 81
Carrot-Apple Waffles 75
Carrot Cake with Creamy Cashew Frosting 277
Cauliflower Turmeric Soup 137
Chocolate-Almond Butter Chia Pudding 63
Chocolate Iced Vanilla Spiced Donut 265
Chocolate Peanut Butter Smoothie Bowl 59
Chocolate-Raspberry Cheesecake 273
Chocolate-Raspberry Chia Cups 269
Citrus & Greens Energizing Smoothie 55
Coconut-Jalapeño Creamed Corn 181
Corn Chowder 129
Creamy Cauliflower Pasta Sauce 207
Creamy Coleslaw with Lemon-Tahini Dressing 177
Dried Fruit & Nut Bites 109
Green Coconut Curry 213
Green Goddess Soup 139
Green Tropical Smoothie 55
Healing Turmeric Smoothie 56
Lavender Latte 263
Lemon-Blueberry Waffles 73
Maple Strawberry & Cream Omega-3 Popsicles 291
Morning Glory Muffins 77
Omega-3 Energy Balls 107
Oven-Roasted Chickpeas & Vegetables 201
Overnight Oats 61
Peanut Butter Chocolate Cookies 287
Raspberry Muffins 275
Roasted Butternut Squash Soup 145
Roasted Heirloom Tomato-Basil Soup 121
Smoothies – Nutrition in a Cup 53
Snickers Energy Balls 107
Spicy Turmeric Cauliflower Tacos 215
Tropical Granola 83
Tropical Popsicles 291
Vegan Cream of Mushroom Soup 133
Warming Turmeric Milk 263
Cod fish
Fish Taco 221
Cookie
Bird's Nest Cookies 289
Breakfast Power Cookies 81
Peanut Butter Chocolate Cookies 287
Raspberry-Chia Thumbprint Cookies 285
Cremini mushroom
Roasted Vegetable Lasagna 241
Vegan Cream of Mushroom Soup 133
Cucumber
Avocado Toast 91
Cauliflower Tabouli 175
Cucumber Basil Lemonade 117
Cucumber Noodle Salad 171
Hearty Rainbow Salad 157
Italian Orzo Salad 199

D

Dates
Bird's Nest Cookies 289
Chocolate-Raspberry Cheesecake 273
Dried Fruit & Nut Bites 109
Lavender Latte 263
Smoothies – Nutrition in a Cup 53
Snickers Energy Balls 107
Donut
Chocolate Iced Vanilla Spiced Donut 265

E

Energy balls
Omega-3 Energy Balls 107
Snickers Energy Balls 107

F

Feta
Baked Eggs in Spicy Tomato Sauce 89
Italian Orzo Salad 199
Orange Beet Kale Salad 155
Flaxseed
Beet Brownies 279
Bird's Nest Cookies 289
Breakfast Power Cookies 81
Carrot-Apple Waffles 75
Chocolate Zucchini Loaf 115
Citrus & Greens Energizing Smoothie 55
Green Tropical Smoothie 55
Healing Turmeric Smoothie 56
Healthy Spelt Banana Bread 111
Omega-3 Energy Balls 107
Raspberry Muffins 275
Smoothies – Nutrition in a Cup 53
Tropical Granola 83

G

Goat cheese
Strawberry, Fennel Salad & Lemony Chia Dressing 163
Green beans
Hearty Minestrone Soup 131
One-Pan Lemon Chicken Bake 225
Sweet & Spicy Green Beans 185

H

Halibut
Crispy Panko Hemp Halibut 229
Fish Taco 221
Hazelnuts
Beet Brownies 279
Massaged Kale Salad with Dijon-Lemon Dressing 165
Orange Beet Kale Salad 155
Hummus
Creamy Vegan Caesar Dressing 159
Roasted Golden Beet Hummus 103
Roasted Red Pepper Hummus 105

K

Kale
Baked Eggs in Spicy Tomato Sauce 89
Braised Cauliflower & Kale 239

Green Goddess Soup 139
Green Tropical Smoothie 55
Hearty Black-Eyed Pea Kale Soup 127
Massaged Kale Salad with Dijon-Lemon Dressing 165
Orange Beet Kale Salad 155
Roasted Vegetable Lasagna 242
Smoothies – Nutrition in a Cup 53
Tomato Lentil Soup 135
Wheat Berry Quinoa Kale Salad 173

L

Lamb
Lamb Shank Curry 259

Lasagna
Roasted Vegetable Lasagna 241

Leek
Creamy Cauliflower Pasta Sauce 207
Green Goddess Soup 139
Hearty Black-Eyed Pea Kale Soup 127
Linguini with Clams 253
Roasted Vegetable Lasagna 241
Vegetable Stock 195

Lettuce
Black Bean & Lentil Burgers 205
Hearty Rainbow Salad 157
Smoothies – Nutrition in a Cup 53
Strawberry, Fennel Salad & Lemony Chia Dressing 163

Linguine
Linguini with Clams 253

Loaf
Blueberry-Lemon Loaf with Yogurt Drizzle 113
Chocolate Zucchini Loaf 115
Pumpkin Ginger Loaf 283

M

Maple syrup
Apple-Pear Quinoa Crumble 271
Avocado Mango Creamsicles 291
Banana-Walnut Muffin 79
Beet Brownies 279
Breakfast Power Cookies 81
Carrot-Apple Waffles 75
Carrot Cake with Creamy Cashew Frosting 277
Cedar Plank Salmon with Maple-Dijon Glaze 231
Chocolate-Almond Butter Cups 267
Chocolate Iced Vanilla Spiced Donut 265
Chocolate-Raspberry Cheesecake 273
Chocolate-Raspberry Chia Cups 269
Creamy Butter Bean Dip 99
Cucumber Basil Lemonade 117
Fall Spiced Granola 85
Healthy Spelt Banana Bread 111
Lemon-Blueberry Waffles 73
Maple Strawberry & Cream Omega-3 Popsicles 291
Maple Turmeric Roasted Rainbow Carrots 191
Morning Glory Muffins 77
Olive Oil Peach Cake 281
Overnight Oats 61
Raspberry-Chia Thumbprint Cookies 285
Ricotta-Pumpkin Pancakes 71
Smoothies – Nutrition in a Cup 53
Tropical Granola 83
Vanilla Pear & Almond-Baked Oatmeal 87

Meatballs
Vegan Marinara Meatballs 251

Muffin
Banana-Walnut Muffin 79
Morning Glory Muffins 77
Raspberry Muffins 275

Mushroom
Hearty Rainbow Salad 157
Lemony Veggie Frittata 219
Roasted Vegetable Lasagna 241
Spicy Turmeric Cauliflower Tacos 215
Vegan Cream of Mushroom Soup 133

O

Oat flour
Banana-Walnut Muffin 79
Breakfast Power Cookies 81
Lemon-Blueberry Waffles 73
Peanut Butter Chocolate Cookies 287
Raspberry-Chia Thumbprint Cookies 285
Spicy Turmeric Cauliflower Tacos 215

P

Parmesan
Baked Spinach & Lemon Risotto 211
Butternut Squash Noodles with Pesto Chicken 223
Creamy Parmesan Brussels Sprouts 183
Crispy Panko Hemp Halibut 229
Hearty Black-Eyed Pea Kale Soup 127
Hearty Minestrone Soup 131
Hemp Seed Basil Pesto 209
Lemony Veggie Frittata 219
Roasted Cauliflower with Hemp Seeds 193
Roasted Vegetable Lasagna 242
Traditional Caesar Dressing 159
Wheat Berry Quinoa Kale Salad 173
Zucchini Summer Pasta 167

Pasta
Creamy Cauliflower Pasta Sauce 207
Hearty Minestrone Soup 131
Linguini with Clams 253
Peanut Butter Pasta 217
Zucchini Summer Pasta 167

Peanut butter
Chocolate Peanut Butter Smoothie Bowl 59
Peanut Butter Chocolate Cookies 287
Peanut Butter Pasta 217
Snickers Energy Balls 107

Pear
Apple-Pear Quinoa Crumble 271
Vanilla Pear & Almond-Baked Oatmeal 87

Peas
Baked Eggs in Spicy Tomato Sauce 89
Fresh Spring Pea Soup 123
Green Coconut Curry 213
Hearty Black-Eyed Pea Kale Soup 127
Hearty Rainbow Salad 157
Mediterranean Quinoa Salad 169
Peanut Butter Pasta 217
Spicy Turmeric Cauliflower Tacos 215
Weeknight Skillet Paella 235

Pecans
Dried Fruit & Nut Bites 109
Fall Spiced Granola 85
Orange Beet Kale Salad 155

Protein
Berry Smoothie Bowl 59
Chocolate Peanut Butter Smoothie Bowl 59
Chocolate Zucchini Loaf 115
Dried Fruit & Nut Bites 109
Protein Banana Blender Pancakes 67
Smoothies – Nutrition in a Cup 53
Snickers Energy Balls 107

Pumpkin
Bird's Nest Cookies 289
Dried Fruit & Nut Bites 109
Fall Spiced Granola 85
Pumpkin Ginger Loaf 283
Pumpkin Marinara Sauce 247
Ricotta-Pumpkin Pancakes 71
Tropical Granola 83
Vegan Marinara Meatballs 251

Q

Quinoa
Apple-Pear Quinoa Crumble 271
Mediterranean Quinoa Salad 169
Turkey Quinoa Meatloaf 255
Wheat Berry Quinoa Kale Salad 173

R

Red bell pepper
Creamy Coleslaw with Lemon-Tahini Dressing 177
Fish Taco 221
Green Coconut Curry 213
Mediterranean Quinoa Salad 169
One-Pan Lemon Chicken Bake 225
Peanut Butter Pasta 217
Pumpkin Marinara Sauce 247
Roasted Vegetable Lasagna 241
Sweet & Spicy Turkey Chili 227

Red lentils
Lemony Lentil Soup 141
Oven-Roasted Chickpeas & Vegetables 201
Tomato Lentil Soup 135

Ricotta cheese
Ricotta-Pumpkin Pancakes 71
Roasted Vegetable Lasagna 242

Rolled oats
Banana-Walnut Muffin 79
Berry-Banana Oat Smoothie 57
Bird's Nest Cookies 289
Breakfast Power Cookies 81
Fall Spiced Granola 85
Omega-3 Energy Balls 107
Overnight Oats 61
Protein Banana Blender Pancakes 67
Tropical Granola 83

S

Salmon
Cedar Plank Salmon with Maple-Dijon Glaze 231
Roasted Salmon with Spinach Chimichurri 233

Sauce
Baked Eggs in Spicy Tomato Sauce 89
Beet Brownies 279
Butternut Squash Noodles with Pesto Chicken 223
Cashew Butternut Squash Alfredo Sauce 249
Cashew Cream Sauce 243
Creamy Cauliflower Pasta Sauce 207
Creamy Parmesan Brussels Sprouts 183
Crispy Panko Hemp Halibut 229
Peanut Butter Pasta 217
Pumpkin Marinara Sauce 247
Roasted Vegetable Lasagna 241
Spicy Turmeric Cauliflower Tacos 215
Sunflower Seed Alfredo Sauce 245
Sweet & Spicy Green Beans 185
Turkey Quinoa Meatloaf 255
Vegan Marinara Meatballs 251

Scones
Blueberry Scones 274

Smoothie
Berry-Banana Oat Smoothie 57
Berry Smoothie Bowl 59
Chocolate Peanut Butter Smoothie Bowl 59
Citrus & Greens Energizing Smoothie 55
Green Tropical Smoothie 55
Healing Turmeric Smoothie 56
Mango Strawberry Pre-Workout Smoothie 55
Seasonal Smoothies 55
Smoothies – Nutrition in a Cup 53

Soup
Cauliflower Turmeric Soup 137
Fresh Spring Pea Soup 123
Green Goddess Soup 139
Hearty Black-Eyed Pea Kale Soup 127
Hearty Minestrone Soup 131
Lemony Lentil Soup 141
Roasted Butternut Squash Soup 145
Roasted Heirloom Tomato-Basil Soup 121
Slow Cooker Tortilla Soup 143
Spiced Carrot-Turmeric Soup 125
Tomato Lentil Soup 135
Vegan Cream of Mushroom Soup 133

Spelt flour
Carrot-Apple Waffles 75
Carrot Cake with Creamy Cashew Frosting 277
Healthy Spelt Banana Bread 111
Lemon-Blueberry Waffles 73
Morning Glory Muffins 77
Pumpkin Ginger Loaf 283
Raspberry-Chia Thumbprint Cookies 285

Spinach
Baked Eggs in Spicy Tomato Sauce 89
Baked Spinach & Lemon Risotto 211
Butternut Squash Noodles with Pesto Chicken 223
Citrus & Greens Energizing Smoothie 55
Green Coconut Curry 213
Green Goddess Soup 139
Oven-Roasted Chickpeas & Vegetables 201
Roasted Salmon with Spinach Chimichurri 233
Roasted Vegetable Lasagna 242
Smoothies – Nutrition in a Cup 53
Strawberry, Fennel Salad & Lemony Chia Dressing 163
Tomato Lentil Soup 135

Strawberry
Mango Strawberry Pre-Workout Smoothie 55
Maple Strawberry & Cream Omega-3 Popsicles 291
Strawberry, Fennel Salad & Lemony Chia Dressing 163
Strawberry Lemonade 117
Tropical Popsicles 291

Sweet corn
Coconut-Jalapeño Creamed Corn 181
Corn & Black Bean Salsa 153
Corn Chowder 129
Sweet & Spicy Turkey Chili 227

Sweet potatoes
Baked Sweet Potato Fries 187
Massaged Kale Salad with Dijon-Lemon Dressing 165

T

Tomato
Baked Eggs in Spicy Tomato Sauce 89
Braised Cauliflower & Kale 239
Butternut Squash Noodles with Pesto Chicken 223
Cauliflower Tabouli 175
Cucumber Noodle Salad 171
Green Coconut Curry 213
Hearty Minestrone Soup 131
Hearty Rainbow Salad 157
Italian Orzo Salad 199
Linguini with Clams 253
Mediterranean Quinoa Salad 169
Pumpkin Marinara Sauce 247
Roasted Heirloom Tomato-Basil Soup 121
Roasted Salmon with Spinach Chimichurri 233
Roasted Vegetable Lasagna 241
Slow Cooker Tortilla Soup 143
Sweet & Spicy Turkey Chili 227
The Best Guacamole 101
Tomato Lentil Soup 135
Tuna Salad Wrap 203
Vegan Marinara Meatballs 251
Weeknight Skillet Paella 235
Zio's Fresh Salsa 97
Zucchini Summer Pasta 167

Tomato paste
Lamb Shank Curry 259
Zio's Fresh Salsa 97

Turkey
Sweet & Spicy Turkey Chili 227
Turkey Quinoa Meatloaf 255

W

Waffles
Carrot-Apple Waffles 75
Lemon-Blueberry Waffles 73

Walnuts
Banana-Walnut Muffin 79
Breakfast Power Cookies 81
Carrot-Apple Waffles 75
Chocolate Zucchini Loaf 115
Dried Fruit & Nut Bites 109
Snickers Energy Balls 107
Strawberry, Fennel Salad & Lemony Chia Dressing 163

Wheat flour
Apple-Cinnamon Multigrain Pancakes 69
Blueberry Scones 274
Chocolate Zucchini Loaf 115
Olive Oil Peach Cake 281

Z

Zucchini
Chocolate Zucchini Loaf 115
Green Goddess Soup 139
Lemony Veggie Frittata 219
Morning Glory Muffins 77
Roasted Salmon with Spinach Chimichurri 233
Roasted Vegetable Lasagna 241
Spiralized Zucchini 149
Zucchini Summer Pasta 167